Crusades

The True and Surprising History of the Crusades

(Legacy of the Catholic Campaign Against the Cathars in France)

Eddie McAvoy

Published By **Jackson Denver**

Eddie McAvoy

All Rights Reserved

Crusades: The True and Surprising History of the Crusades (Legacy of the Catholic Campaign Against the Cathars in France)

ISBN 978-1-77485-658-1

No part of this guidebook shall be reproduced in any form without permission in writing from the publisher except in the case of brief quotations embodied in critical articles or reviews.

Legal & Disclaimer

The information contained in this ebook is not designed to replace or take the place of any form of medicine or professional medical advice. The information in this ebook has been provided for educational & entertainment purposes only.

The information contained in this book has been compiled from sources deemed reliable, and it is accurate to the best of the Author's knowledge; however, the Author cannot guarantee its accuracy and validity and cannot be held liable for any errors or omissions. Changes are periodically made to this book. You must consult your doctor or get professional medical advice before using any of the suggested remedies, techniques, or information in this book.

Upon using the information contained in this book, you agree to hold harmless the Author from and against any damages, costs, and expenses, including any legal fees potentially resulting from the application of any of the information provided by this guide. This disclaimer applies to any damages or injury caused by the use and application, whether directly or indirectly, of any advice or information presented, whether for breach of contract, tort, negligence, personal injury, criminal intent, or under any other cause of action.

You agree to accept all risks of using the information presented inside this book. You need to consult a professional medical practitioner in order to ensure you are both able and healthy enough to participate in this program.

Table Of Contents

Introduction 1

Chapter 1: The First Crusade 5

Chapter 2: The Holy Land 25

Chapter 3: The Aftermath From The First Crusade 44

Chapter 4: The Myths Of The Crusades .. 54

Chapter 5: The Second Crusade 64

Chapter 6: The Siege Of Damascus (And Lisbon) 82

Chapter 7: The King's Crusade 93

Chapter 8: One Crusade Is Over; Another One Begins 112

Chapter 9: The Fifth Crusade 134

Introduction

It is believed that there have been 268 years of peace between humankind's beginnings and the present. It doesn't take very long to notice how much warfare humanity has engaged with when we look back at human history. It seemed like they were fighting one another from the very beginning of time.

We will be taking a look into the Middle Ages. This is the most turbulent period in European history. We will examine the Crusades from different eras and present the Seven Major Crusades. We will try to dispel some of the myths associated with the Crusades as well as give an accurate picture of the motivations, purpose, consequences, and outcomes of the Crusades.

What are your thoughts when Crusade appears? Perhaps you think of brutality committed in defense of religion. Perhaps you envision noble knights or heroic deeds being done for God. The modern world has made Crusade an offensive word. This is because it is often used to disparage the Middle East and West. We are trying to offer a neutral, balanced and critical look at Crusades in the hopes of being able show you exactly what happened.

Before we dive into the history that preceded the Crusades', we have to first define what a Crusade means. Historians have yet to come up with a satisfactory definition for Crusade because so many people in history started their own "crusades." Some historians think that Crusades were religious campaigns that were supported by the Pope. Some historians view the Crusades as a set of major military campaign in Levant. This is where Jerusalem was. Crusades would fall under this category. We will therefore be covering military campaigns that liberated Jerusalem and secured the Holy Land from Muslim troops.

We aim to give you a clear summary of the Seven Crusades, as well as an objective, honest look at those who took the Cross in an attempt to win favor and glory from God. We will explore the various myths associated with the Crusade along with the reception by Muslims of the Crusade. This presentation will be viewed through the lense of European forces that were involved in the series of wars. We will go from the Crusade's beginnings through the last few major crusades.

We hope that this book will give you an excellent overview of the Crusades and provide you with a new perspective on the truths surrounding them. Modern history has begun to view this time period with a revisionist eye. Unfortunately, there is much misinformation in relation to the

Crusades. Our goal to empower and educate you is to make it possible for you to see the period from a deeper understanding of its political, religious, as well as military nature. Let's start with the Byzantine Empire, which is the very beginning of the Crusade.

Chapter 1: The First Crusade

First, it is important to consider the history of Medieval Europe, as well as the influence and motivations of First Crusade.

There was a lot of fighting in the Middle East. Seljuk Turks came to power in a bid to take over Byzantine-controlled territories. These Islamic forces had quickly moved to the Middle East, and they pushed into Levant. They would then come up against Byzantine troops, decimating them in a huge battle called the Battle of Manzikert.

The Battle of Manzikert

The Battle of Manzikert witnessed a fierce battle between Seljuk Turks as well as the Byzantine armies in Asia Minor. To give context to the battle, it's helpful to recall the events that led up to it. Alp Arslan the leader of Seljuk Turks had been waging a civil war against Byzantines but his current interest in conquest was aimed at the Egyptian leadership. Romanos IV was the Byzantine Emperor and had reached a deal with Alp to end their fighting.

Alp had agreed to these terms too quickly, and preferred to confront the Fatimid Caliphate, which is the Islamic Caliphate located in Egypt. Alp was not the loser in the agreement. His forces had seized a substantial portion of territory which included Armenia. Romanos wanted it back.

The Byzantine Emperor did not care much about long-term peace. In fact, he used peace treaty as a trick to fool the Seljuks in to lowering their guards. Romanos was aware that the Turks would not suspect any attack and assembled a military army to lead them onwards to recover their Armenian territory.

Romanos' attempt to recapture their territory was not without its faults. Andronicus DUCAS, his political rival and fellow-emperor, came with him. Ducas was at war with Romanos. It was clear that Ducas didn't have the heart to support the emperor. He underestimated the strenuous journey that lay ahead of him. They had to travel quite a distance before they reached their destination. Furthermore, there were several instances of soldiers working in the streets to plunder innocent villages.

Romanos did not employ highly trained soldiers to their ranks. The Byzantines, however, chose to use primarily a small mercenary force in order to maintain control over the forces and not react to the changing political climate. The battle would make it clear that Mercenaries didn't have any natural loyalty to their employers.

Romanos had to be vigilant because of the low quality soldiers, the long travel distances involved and the rival Romanos had to watch. It was hard to believe their loss at Manzikert. In the belief that Alp, Turkey's leader, would be far away, the Byzantine forces marched to Manzikert. The idea that Turkish forces would notice their army tearing though the countryside was something they managed to ignore. Soon word reached Alp Arslan of the Byzantines having violated the terms of their peace deal.

Romanos was unaware that the Seljuk army had sent its full force towards his direction. Combine that with poor scouting, and he was in for a lot of trouble when he got to Manzikert. Romanos realized quickly that he was facing off against the leader Seljuk's forces as the Sultan's troops surrounded them.

Romanos, on the other hand, was keen to win the battle and retake his land.

The battle was bloody, as both forces clashed. They engaged in several skirmishes despite having large forces on each side. The Seljuks soon proved their ability to use hit and run tactics, which was quickly proven by them. Romanos continued to issue commands. But his loyalty towards Andronicus proved fatal. At a critical moment Andronicus ordered every unit to leave the battle. Romanos' forces were surrounded and cut off from any reinforcements. The battle was short-lived.

Romanos, now humiliated and defeated was dragged in front of the Sultan. Here, the Sultan placed his foot upon Romanos's face, and told him that it was okay. After that, he was released. Romanus had also lost complete control of his home forces and soon the Byzantine Imperial had erupted in large civil war. Rome, once a great nation, was reduced to a few infights.

This was the moment historians all agree that the Byzantine Emperor's decline began. It was impossible to control the expansion of Islamic Military forces into Europe after the Empire's core strength was destroyed. They were now free to conquer.

The Council of Clermont

As the Seljuk Turks grew in Europe, threatening Nicaea as well, Pope Urban was confronted with the task of governing a Christian world split. The papacy, which was once strong and respected by many Christian nations in Europe, had fallen prey to infighting. The Church's authority has been weakened by several schisms and their authority is not as broad as it once was. This presented an opportunity for Alexius Comnenos to become the Emperor of Byzantine.

Alexius had sent his envoy, to meet with Pope Urban and request help in fighting back Turkish forces. Pope Urban saw this as an opportunity to unite members of the church, to bring in fighting Christian forces together, and unite them with a common enemy.

Pope Urban called to a large meeting the clergy. He invited them to gather and listen to the message. He gave a warning about Islamic forces, who have taken control of Eastern churches and are trying to execute the clergy.

He asked that the forces unite and make war on those who threaten them. Pope Urban demanded unification of the church, submission to papacy, as well as the surrender of many sinners he saw for their actions against their Christian brothers. In return, he offered forgiveness and participation in this new conflict. Loudly screaming "Deus Vult!" - God Wills It!, the Pope stated that there was no need to fight each other anymore.

The Pope then traveled to France, where he preached about the crusade. Pope Urban, a man of strategy, had already secured two major alliances from the French nobility. These nobles were quick to support his cause, giving it instant legitimacy.

The peasantry listened loudly to the Pope's call. They responded rapidly to the message faster than anyone expected and rallied behind the leader. Then they began to prepare for their pilgrimage into the Holy Land, which would involve violence to defend Jerusalem from the Turkish threat.

While the Pope would eventually continue to train a professional military in order to counter the threat, the common folk had an entirely different idea. People's Crusade arose from the ideology, perhaps because it offered the possibility of glory or plunder.

Peter the Hermit arose before the official start of the first Formal Crusade.

Peter was a poor priest. He claimed that during his trip to the Holy Land, the Seljuk Turks rebuffed him and that he couldn't enter the Holy Land to finish his pilgrimage. It is not known where Peter was at the time that the Pope first called for the Crusades. But once he heard the message, it became his and he began to passionately advocate for it.

Peter the Hermit was an aesthetic. A man committed to living a minimalistic life, his dress reflected this. Peter, who was wearing a simple gown and riding on the backs of donkeys, had a dream to bring the war to the Turks. He had a knack for emotionality, his words could make people scream and soon he was in the company of many peasants that wanted to fight against the Turkish forces who had occupied Jerusalem.

Peter was their leader and the People's Crusade began from that moment. Although their ranks were large, they were very poor, extremely unmotivated and, for the most part, unarmed. They were able to march boldly towards Holy Land despite their lack in weapons and expertise.

They quickly became a nuisance, raiding innocent villages for food. The Emperor was dissatisfied that they had to take care of a large population of untrained rabble. When they were unable to sustain themselves, he offered them transport across the sea to reach Turkish land in order to eliminate the peasants from his food stores.

When they arrived in Asia Minor, chaos ensued. Different factions in this group began to argue over methodology and they split in haste. Peter had been warned not to engage with military activity by the Emperor of Byzantines. But his control was compromised. The People's Crusade pushed on, seizing control of Xerigordon and gaining Turkish territory.

Peter had returned to Constantinople for more supplies and to secure additional forces. But he was never seen again. This is mainly because when the Turkish military force saw that the People's Crusade was moving into their territory, the Turkish military quickly took control of the town and brutally executed all the crusaders responsible for Xerigordon.

The rest of the force was tricked into moving towards Nicaea to meet the Turkish army. The Turkish soldiers quickly attacked the army of People's Crusade and decimated it. The majority of the people were killed while the survivors were either captured or liberated in an ambush by the Byzantine Army's main forces.

Peter, having lost most his forces, went on to support Crusade.

The People's Crusade's disastrous attempt was a setback that led to the First Crusade's actual movements. The Crusade didn't consist of one large campaign. It also did not have all the same origin military forces. They were more like a collection of troops who fought under the banners different nobles. Let's examine the profile of each major leader of the First Crusade.

Godfrey from Boullion

Godfrey was a nobleman. He quickly raised an army, and brought his brothers to the Holy Land to assist him in his efforts to free it from the enemy. Many looked up and considered him the best candidate to lead Crusade. He didn't assume full leadership of Crusade as it was made up of four different armies each marching in a separate direction but were directed toward the Holy Land.

His forces were not huge and, although he was involved in many battles throughout the wars, Godfrey did not take a central role in the final battles to Jerusalem. After reaching Jerusalem, his reputation was enhanced and he led an attack into the city. After Jerusalem was secured, he became the ruler of Jerusalem.

Raymond of Toulouse

Raymond of Toulouse, an English prince, was the first person to acknowledge the

Pope's call. He was a strong Christian and wanted the fight for his faith. Thus he joined arms, raised his army and marched towards Holy Land. He would then claim his fame in Antioch. Here they attacked the city and captured a holy artifact. It was a miracle that would inspire many of those who fought.

Adhemar, Le Puy

Adhemar was a bishop that had served as a companion to the Pope during Crusades. He also led troops towards the Holy Land with many of his fellow soldiers. Adhemar was the Pope's representative. He also had a flair for warfare, serving often alongside the troops. He stayed at Raymond of Toulouse, and was faithful to the spiritual needs the soldiers. He had already made the pilgrimage up to Jerusalem. This makes him an ideal candidate to assist with navigating troops to their destination.

Bohemond The I:

Bohemond I, a prince, was an integral leader in the First Crusade. His leadership was outstanding. As a professional warman, he had a vast knowledge of how to lead troops. He had a deep sense of piety.

Bohemond didn't initially participate in the Crusades. However, while he waged war on Italy, Bohemond noticed that there was a constant stream of Crusaders passing though, all heading to Constantinople to fight against the Turkish troops. Bohemond was probably motivated not by faith but conquest. So he quickly accepted the offer to join them. He would play a central role in First Crusade. He also led the soldiers across Asia Minor. It was a remarkable feat.

These leaders all shared one common cause: taking back Jerusalem, and pushing back Muslim conquerors. Each of the leaders made their own way to Constantinople. There, Emperor Alexius demanded they all swear fealty towards him and take an oath stating that all conquered territories would be returned back to Byzantine. The agreement was made by everyone, but the words proved to be only polite gestures.

Let's jump to the next section and look at Nicaea. This is the first engagement in a series of crucial actions on the road towards the Holy Land.

Nicaea is where the Crusader Army's might was tested. Godfrey and his companions reached the city first and found it extremely well fortified. The city was so well fortified that they were unable to resist the temptation to seize it and force their enemies to flee. Although tension was present due to the lack of a military force from the Seljuk Turks, everyone was concerned about whether Kilij Aranslan, the current ruler, would aid them.

They held the town hostage for eight days. However, it was not enough. Bohemond didn't arrive until then, so no formal strategy was established.

Nicaea is more than just a village. It was also one of the key bases of Kilij. This location was rich in treasure, so capturing it would be a serious blow to their enemies. The crusaders' desire to strike a blow were motivating the princes into forming a council. This council would allow them the traditional siege warfare to break through enemy lines.

Alexius watched over the construction of the trebuchets, and the council at large. From a distance Alexius waited and observed, having secretly prepared conditions for the Byzantines to retake control of the city.

As the soldiers began to prepare for the siege they were accosted by two Turkish spies. After interrogation it was discovered that Sultan Kilij was indeed on his path to repel Crusading troops. In fact, with a massive army and ready to fight, he had been planning to launch another counter-attack the day before.

This was Kilij's first major clash in the First Crusade. At this time, Kilij would realize just how huge the Crusade's forces really were. He led his soldiers into the war against crusaders. Unfortunately, the sheer numbers of soldiers against his army was more than he was ready to handle. He was willing to fight the intruders after he had accepted the pleas from the Turkish soldiers encamped inside Nicaea. Their tenacity surprised him. After a series of battles, Sultan's forces were defeated and he fled. After this, he didn't go back to

Nicaea. He left the besieged Turks with the task of managing things.

The battles for the city grew more intense each day as both sides waged war. The Crusaders attempted to break through walls with their arrows and ballistas but the Nicaean Turkeys kept firing at them. The siege continued on for weeks without success, until finally a cunning plan came to fruition. Alexius had grown tired of waiting for the defenses to fall. For nearly five weeks the siege went on without any progress. They were mistakenly led to believe that the Byzantine main Army had arrived. This made their wills crumble.

Alexius took advantage Turks fear and negotiated peace. This allowed him to take control of Nicaea. His forces were tiny compared to Crusader troops, but they secured the city. Alexius was clever and took all the money. He wasn't foolish, however. He made payments to the leaders, as well as the soldiers, who were involved in the siege and paid them for the effort.

After five weeks of starving, starving and bleeding in the city, this action was not well received by Crusading arms. They hadn't intended to return Nicaea but this was seen as an act a bit of underhandedness on the Emperor's part. Alexius made repartee as best he could, but the rift that was growing there was not going to be fixed.

The Crusaders, despite not being able to take the territory they were holding, were happy with their victory. They not only had defeated Kilij but had also stolen his treasure and caused the Sultan to lose his face across his territory. After they captured this high-value target, the Crusaders armed and assembled their forces before moving on to Antioch.

Chapter 2: The Holy Land

With Nicaea secure, the Crusaders moved to Antioch in order to be able to seize the city before their last movements to Jerusalem. For Palestine to gain entry, the key was taking control of Antioch. Jerusalem was too secure for Crusaders not to be able attack it without a crucial base of operations. If the Crusaders wanted to secure Holy Land they would need to overtake Antioch.

This caused a serious problem for Crusaders. Their force had been dispersed on the way to Antioch and was now at a reduced capacity. Additionally, Antioch was more massive and fortified then Nicaea. The city, which was founded in the 6th-century, had been under Byzantine control since 969. The Byzantines increased the defenses and built fortresses to make it hard to attack. Both the captures of the city were the result cleverly employed of spies, treachery, and not a direct assault.

But, the Crusaders couldn't resist taking the city. It was the portal to Palestine and home of the Holy Place of Jerusalem. They arrived just after Nicaea's capture in 1097. They knew the siege wouldn't be short. But the truth was, this Siege would go down as one of the longest sieges and most well-known in history.

It was evident that a direct assault on the city would have been a suicide attempt upon reaching it. The fortresses of the city were much too fortified. It was impossible to conquer the city with one-on-one force. Instead, Crusading forces set up camp near the enemy territory and began cutting off the supply to the city.

The enemy forces noticed quickly that the Crusaders didn't intend to make an immediate attack, so they devised a counterattack strategy using harassment. To keep the Crusaders from being too close to the walls of the fortresses the Turks used the cavalry of their soldiers and the ranged soldiers of their soldiers to harass them and push them back.

One funny story from the Siege saw enemy forces attacking Raymond, Toulouse while other parties were busy scavenging for supplies. Raymond's troops were able to adequately organize to repel the terrorists and drive them away. Raymond ordered his troops to follow and chase the Turkish forces in the dark. As they crossed the bridge, one of Crusaders horses got scared, throwing him off. The whole pursuing army was in panic and fell back, afraid of being ambushed.

The siege continued despite many Crusaders personnel starving due to a lack of supplies. The walls were just too high to reach and, as weeks went by the siege started to look less likely.

Yaghi Siyan led a large army that arrived in February several months after the siege began. This force was able to stop the siege. Crusaders then found themselves fighting fiercely against the reinforcements of the enemy. The fighting was hard and bloody but, in the end the Crusaders triumphed over their enemy, forcing them to retreat. The siege would keep going.

Bohemond was now able to use his cunning skills to take control of Antioch. Bohemond was able to contact an Antioch guard, who was looking over one tower of the wall. Bohemond was able convince the guard to cooperate with him to open Antioch's doors, possibly in exchange for money and/or other favors. Bohemond presented his plan to the other leaders. He demanded that he receive leadership of

Antioch for breaking the siege. It wasn't something the other leaders liked at first but they became more desperate as the situation worsened. They had to act fast. The word got out that another army was in their midst.

Kerbogha, an experienced soldier who had gathered a large force of soldiers to rescue Antioch was just days away. The threat of being confronted by another army while they were in an unsafe position motivated them all to agree to let Bohemond rule the city.

Bohemond along with the Crusading units gathered at the Tower of the Two Sisters during the night and waited for the gates of Kerbogha. A small group of Crusaders were allowed to climb the Tower's walls.

The next set of decisions was unheroic. After they were allowed entry, the Crusaders began to massacre thousands of people. Antioch was in turmoil as they murdered anyone who opposed them. Many Christian citizens in Antioch were also massacred.

The Crusading army had to deal with Kerbogha's army shortly after they captured Antioch. After months and months of siege, the Crusaders had finally captured Antioch. Now they had to keep it.

The Turkish leader, as Crusading units prepared to battle Kerbogha for their supremacy, had his own problems. His ambitions were enormous and he used many factions to build his army. Kerbogha was at the time the leader these factions. He was worried that if Antioch became their leader, he would be determined to conquer all of the faction's territories. This led to bickering, suspicion and infighting among the leaders.

As Crusaders began to feel a loss of morale, they were under siege. Many soldiers started to feel tired from the siege, which was accompanied by a lack of food and the threat of losing it. Before the capture of Antioch, desertion was already a regular occurrence. It continued inside the walls of Antioch. A single discovery, however, changed the tide and lifted the soldiers' morale.

Peter Bartholomew - a man without any real importance - had been digging through the temple ruin and found a lance. The vision of Saint Andrew, Bartholomew claimed, had given him the idea of the spear. This legendary artifact is known as the Holy Lance. This Lance was used to pierce Jesus Christ's side following his crucifixion. It was a holy Relic. Adhemar, a majority of the clergy, was skeptical about the authenticity of Relic. But many soldiers were thrilled by the prospect and celebrated it. It seemed to excite soldiers and remind them that God was with their side in the coming battle to repel Kerbogha's men. With such enthusiasm, leadership seized the opportunity to place Raymond of Aguiler as their historian at the front lines carrying the spear and standard.

The Battle of Antioch took effect within a month of Antioch being captured. Kerbogha's forces were ready to meet them, but the Turkish commander had underestimated the Crusaders' size. Kerbogha was defeated and then abandoned by his own forces. Many of these had tactically pulled back to stop Kerbogha taking control of Antioch. Kerbogha suffered a terrible fight, and his army was destroyed that day.

Kerbogha fleeing, and the remaining resistance surrendering to Bohemond, Antioch was liberated. After a nine-month battle, one of most brutal sieges in history was over. The Crusaders won and were now able to gain entry into Palestine and travel towards the Holy Land.

Bohemond held on to the city's control despite Raymond and Godfrey being opposed. Bohemond secured allies and enough troops to hold on to the city, and there was much contention. However, he argued that he could be the leader. Raymond of Toulouse became the official commander in the charge against Jerusalem. Bohemond felt content with where he was currently at. Bohemond had no desire to move ahead but the others moved on from the city and headed for the Holy Land.

Raymond of Toulouse had left Antioch to seek control of Tripoli. Peter Bartholomew continued the discussion on visions of Saint Andrew giving him instructions, and

Raymond was clearly in control over the Holy Artifact.

The Crusaders were now divided, with Godfrey feeling reticent to recognize Raymond as their official head, but continuing along the general course of Raymond's trip. Raymond had come to Arqah hoping to take control. Arqah had at the time strategic importance due to its proximity with Tripoli's roads. Raymond intended to seize control of the roads in order to ensure trade routes were secure and supplies would not be allowed into the city.

Raymond did not realize how difficult the siege on Arqah would be and quickly got involved in the fight. Previously, the rulers in towns and villages didn't fight with Crusader troops. Instead they paid tribute and allowed Raymond to go ahead without issue. Arqah, however, had no desire to surrender.

Godfrey (and Robert) arrived to assist Raymond, but the siege continued on for many months. Peter Bartholomew also claimed that Saint Andrew had told Raymond that he must attack the city with his forces.

A few months after Adhemar's death from the plague, the Crusaders were experiencing a high spiritual temperature. There was tension in the camp and Raymond was put in difficult circumstances by Peter's continual claims of divine wisdom. Peter's last vision was openly condemned and a heated argument ensued. Peter claimed that God would help him by giving him a trial through fire.

Peter Bartholomew was able to walk through the walls after the camp agreed to his demands. He claimed an angel would protect him, which would support his authority on the subject of his visions. He ran between the flaming logs and was badly burned. Bartholomew suffered severe pain in his body and spent the final days of his life in bedridden, in extreme agony, unable even to walk. Bartholomew died from his wounds. The Spear to Longinus (the Holy Spear) was proved to have been a fabrication. Peter's spirit authority died with them.

Raymond continued his journey after the siege on Arqah ended. Most cleverly, the Emir (or ruler of Tripoli) sent an emissary carrying gifts to Raymond. This was sufficient bribe for the Crusaders to abandon siege to the city. They marched forward, toward Jerusalem.

Their forces were no longer as powerful as they once had been. Although their numbers were large at the beginning of Crusade, historians differ widely about the size. But it is common knowledge that the First Crusade's force was one of Europe's largest. Their force had fallen to 12,000 soldiers by then. Although the force was large enough to sustain a siege in enemy territory for a prolonged period of time, it was not enough.

After months of walking, they finally reached Holy Land. They had reached Jerusalem. Things got much more complicated after that. The Seljuk Turks, who had lost control to the city's enemies, the Fatimid Egyptian force, meant that Crusaders faced an entirely different enemy than the Turks. The Crusaders desired peace and the Fatimids tried to broker it with Latin forces. However, their terms required Jerusalem to remain as it was. These conditions weren't met and the Crusaders kept pushing forward for Jerusalem.

Jerusalem was not an easy location to invade. It was difficult because the city was in a desert area without the natural resources necessary to sustain a sieging force made it difficult to seize it. Iftikhar, the commander, secured enough supplies to keep the city under siege. Iftikhar also kicked Christians out, to ensure there would be no betrayals in the walls. After Iftikhar's efforts in protecting the city and realizing that it would be a disaster if the Fatimid Caliphate reacted with a formal army, to repel the Crusaders then the Crusaders tried to storm the city.

Because Jerusalem's walls were strong enough to withstand the assault, it was unsuccessful. The Crusaders were going to need to use siege weapons in order to defeat their enemy. The Crusaders were more limited because of the Egyptian forces' clearing of Jerusalem. This made it difficult for them to gather wood to construct siege engines.

Crusaders lost their strength as they tried to build war machines by gathering wood and water. This was not an easy process and they learned that the Egyptian army was approaching. This knowledge caused panic in the Crusaders. If they weren't able to secure Jerusalem, they would soon be caught by an army in foreign territory.

The siege engines were built from wood they had gathered from distant places, and wood taken from ships that had arrived to support Crusading troops. They were equipped with ladders and siege towers to capture Jerusalem.

The fighting was fierce but they were able, with quick determination and clever use of one the siege Towers as a diversion to their forces, to secure enough territory to invade. The siege tower was designed so that soldiers could not be injured by arrows. Additionally, ladders were attached to the wall which would allow forces from the tower to quickly reach the wall and take control. Once the forces have been inside the walls the battle will be more about getting the gates open for the main troops.

The siege-towers made their way up Jerusalem's walls, allowing Raymond and Godfrey's troops positions to enter the city. Although fighting was fierce, Godfrey was able lead his forces and seize the main gate. This opened Jerusalem to the main fight. The swarms were able to flood into Jerusalem and take the fighting to its core.

The battle lasted almost all night, but at the end of it all the governor surrendered. Their ultimate goal was to take control of the city. After their capture, there was a massacre in the city. This was a horrific and brutal affair. While medieval armies were known to commit suicide after capturing a city for their own purposes, the brutality of this killing spree has been deemed to be particularly brutal.

The Crusaders are the only ones left within the city after the slaughter. Any Jew or Muslim civilians were massacred, and only the Crusaders remained. Raymond of Toulouse offered the title and was interested in the position. He believed Christ was king of Jerusalem. He would not overthrow his Lord-and-Savior.

Godfrey had similar concerns. However, he stated that he would become the Advocate of Holy Sepulcher. A title that means that he was actually the ruling authority of a city but that he was ruling it for his liege. To prevent him being accused, Godfrey became furious at Godfrey's attempt to take control of the city. Raymond was angered by Godfrey's boldness in taking control of the town and he took his forces with him and fled the area, leaving the other leaders alone to deal a new threat: the Egyptian forces.

Fatimid ambassadors reached Jerusalem and ordered Crusaders go. They didn't want to fight against Latin troops at the moment. They had accepted the Crusaders previous exploits in capturing control of Syria, but they wanted Levant control where Jerusalem was. Godfrey began preparing his forces for battle against the advancing army that was headed towards Jerusalem.

This army was much bigger than the Crusaders' forces. Fatimid forces had approximately 50,000 members, far more than the Crusaders. This size was quite intimidating for Crusaders, however they had no choice. Instead of risking siege, they rallied their forces, and marched out towards Ascalon to meet the Fatimid forces.

Although the Fatimids had a large number of troops, they were not nearly as powerful and ruthless as the Seljuk Turks.

The Crusaders marched into the enemy encampment ahead of the enemy's heavy cavalry and caused serious fighting between the two sides. In chaos, al-Afdal (the leader) called for a retreat, being surprised by how strong and coordinated the Crusaders were, and he fled to Ascalon.

The Crusaders had spent the night in preparation to invade Ascalon, finishing off their opponent. But intelligence soon advised them that al Afdal their enemy, had loaded up his forces onto a transport, and retreated into Egypt. This was a decisive victory of the Crusaders which would secure their victory over Jerusalem. After a lengthy campaign and a series of setbacks as well as downsides, they finally won the First Crusade. Jerusalem was theirs. The vow to save the Holy City was fulfilled. The First Crusade achieved success.

Chapter 3: The Aftermath from the First Crusade

One of the biggest impacts of The First Crusade was the establishment Crusader countries. These states were the County and Kingdom of Jerusalem, the Principality and Antioch. These states were very small but had great influence in establishing Crusading strength.

The first Crusade's successes would inspire many more Crusades. They also prove to be a useful tool for political leaders who wish to motivate the people to become soldiers. Many of those who returned to their homeland after the Crusades became heroes, and the Crusade concept was widely romanticized by writers. The First Crusade represented a strong image, showing a knight who takes up arms in order to repel the enemy. This would help to motivate other Crusaders.

After the first crusade, there was a minor crusade that began in 1101. This became the Crusade of 1101, or the Crusade of the Faint Hearted. The name of this minor action is because many people who had departed the First Crusade decided to take it on. Why? Because they could not keep their Crusader Vow, and they would be excommunicated.

After Jerusalem had been secured and the Crusader countries established, it quickly became clear that these small state were within easy reach of many different power and that the Seljuk Turks posed a threat. The Crusaders were far removed from any major source to provide reinforcements. Now is the time to protect what the First Crusade has fought so hard to secure.

Many people were instructed by the Archbishop in Milan to preach for the people to carry the Cross and defend the territory. There was also a renewed threat to excommunication for those who didn't fulfill their Crusader promise. This helped enough people rally for the Holy Land.

Spirits were high as the first Crusade was such a success. It was now time for the Crusaders, to move on and seize control of the territory.

The armies were less coordinated than they were in the First Crusade. Lombards (Burgundians), Bavarians and others who weren't familiar with the First Crusade were among those in the ranks. These forces moved independently towards the Holy Land. Many of them acted exactly as the People's Crusade did, causing property damage and destruction.

Most importantly, the details regarding the goals and objectives of these armies were a little unclear. Many were unable to see the big picture and the Archbishop who was appointed to oversee them was almost completely ignored by both leader, soldier, and commander. Many of them longed to win wars, to plunder the land and to receive praise for their actions. However, none of them had a coherent plan for their next steps.

The Lombards were immediately enraged by Emperor Alexius when they arrived in Byzantine land. Alexius helped them get to Nicomedia. The Lombardians did not invade Asia Minor, but waited for reinforcements.

While they waited, word reached them that Bohemond the newly crowned Prince d'Antioch had been captured and taken by the Danishmends. Crusaders thought that they needed to rescue the man they had led in the First Crusade's charge. Once they reached Nicomedia, they made a plan for marching on Niskar, where Bohemond was still being held.

There was much disagreement over whether the Crusaders should go or wait for more reinforcements. But the final decision was to go. They would join forces and advance, liberating their captured comrades, then moving on into the Holy Land.

Kilij Arkslan had learned a lot through his interactions in the First Crusade. He had discovered that his greatest weakness during this time was the disjointedness of surrounding regions and infighting. He made sure to unify them so that they could all cooperate to defeat the Crusaders. After hearing that the army was moving forward and forming alliances, he prepared his troops to attack these new enemies.

First, the Turks started to harass the Crusaders during their journey toward Niskar. This was done by picking at their defenses as well as providing constant pressure that caused permanent damage for the traveling soldiers. The Crusaders captured Ancyra and were forced to flee because Kilij's forces were continually attacking them.

The Lombards refused be discouraged and demanded they keep moving towards Niskar. It was there that the Turks met them at Mersivan's mountains. The Turks had worked hard at steering the Crusaders into this land. But they were quickly at a disadvantage. The Turks found this area ideal, because it was dry and dusty without supplies for Crusaders. The land was also extremely wide, making it ideal terrain for cavalry charge.

The Crusaders became outmatched quickly on the first day. The Turks spread fighting over several days, cutting the one advancing army out of the rest. This forced them into open warfare, resulting in the German soldiers losing quickly. Crusaders surrounded them completely, and this caused morale to plummet. The Crusaders tried to fight their way back, and they fought bravely, but the Turks simply had overwhelming numbers and an amazing strategy.

As the days passed, the chances of winning this war diminished. Many Crusaders fled after it became evident that they were on losing side of the battle. The Lombards tried their best to fight but were quickly defeated. The French, German, and British forces were forced to retreat, but the Turks attacked, reducing as many as they can. Their forces were nearly destroyed in just four days. Those who managed escape fled their homelands.

Some other forces arrived in addition to the main Crusader force, but they were all soon under Kilij's control. Kilij realized that it would be much easier to press ahead and confront these armies as they approached his territory. Then, they were crushed quickly before they could get into the land.

William of Nevers was originally planning to accompany his army and catch up to the Lombards on his arrival. Soon, it was clear that he wouldn't be able keep up with the Lombards' pace. He decided to attempt to capture the City of Iconium.

However, the city was difficult to capture. The area was quite hostile and difficult for people who aren't familiar with these lands. William was not able to take over the city. William then moved on south through the desert south of Heraclea to try and take control of the city. He was soon attacked by Turks. They pursued him with great determination and fury. His forces were quickly killed and only a few people, including himself managed to survive the onslaught.

It became obvious that this crusade was going to be different from the last. The First Crusade may have been a major affair that saw a large force capable fighting off the Sultan and taking many cities under his control, but each force of the minor crusade arrived quickly in foreign lands.

The fates for the Bavarians were much like those of other Crusaders. As a group with other nobles such as Hugh IX of Aquitaine or William IX, the Bavarian Prince Welf led their forces towards Heraclea. Kilij quickly overtook them.

Those who had survived the losses eventually reached Antioch. Many decided that it was better to go home than to suffer humiliation or suffering from defeat.

The Crusade at 1101 ended all momentum gained by the First Crusade, and the Crusade at 1101 completely destroyed the Crusaders. These armies had been defeated with such speed that they hadn't made it to Holy Land before Kilij slain them with brutality and speed. This allowed him the opportunity to maximize his power, and to capitalize on the fact Turks would be more able to resist foreign invaders if they had a stronger sense for unity.

There was a lot of blame among the Crusaders for their actions, with the Crusaders accusing the Byzantines. The mood toward a Crusade rapidly cooled at this point. It wouldn't happen again until nearly fifty-years later.

Before we begin to look at The Second Crusade, let us first review some of the myths associated with the Crusades.

Chapter 4: The Myths of the Crusades

The Crusades are a series that involved major wars motivated by complex ideas and concepts. They are also quite flexible. One can use the Crusades as a topic however they wish. For instance, if someone wants to prove the evils in Christianity, they only need to mention the Crusades. The Crusades could be used to demonstrate how Muslims were violent conquerors. Anyone can make a point about the Crusades by using it. This is a common topic in just about every historical discussion.

Let's not forget to mention some myths which are often presented as fact and could cause people to believe things that were wrong about the Crusades.

Myth 1. The Crusades were an act de aggression against innocent Muslims

As we've seen earlier, the First Crusades are a defensive and not aggressive war. The First Crusade's primary purpose was to unify soldiers in a common cause against an enemy, not to conquer against innocent civilians.

It's crucial to recognize the current times. It's easy to imagine our current social value system being transported to Medieval Europe. We can then be horrified at the crimes committed back then. However, we must also remember that our values differed from theirs. The way of life was war until recently for nearly every culture. The Seljuk Turks attempted to conquer their enemies and fight the Fatimid Caliphate. Christian rulers and nobles raised armies, and fought endlessly for power. Conquest and war were a part and parcel of human life back in those days. Although it may seem horrible to us, they knew how it worked.

It does not excuse them from their atrocities. The age's wickedness and crimes are not to be forgotten. But it is important for us to see the past in this way. The Crusades were no less heinous than any other war, whatever the reason. It is absurd to single out Crusades' actions against an enemy who was as violent as they were, and then claim that the Seljuk Turks weren't guilty. These nations were involved in significant warfare. The control of cities was frequently transferred. These armies conquered whatever their motivations and became part of our way of life.

Of course, it's important to distinguish between innocents who were not involved in the war and those who fought. Attacks on innocent observers or the plundering by those not involved are tragic, there is no doubt about that. The acts of violence against the individual were committed on both ends and were not excused.

Myth #2: The Crusaders are Heroic Defenders of Faith.

Although it's possible that faith motivated many Crusaders, most were motivated by survival. Many men participated in Crusades because they were hungry, unemployed, or simply wanted to be able to support their families through famine. While some men saw the Crusades as a way to make money or get treasure, others saw the crusades as a way to do the right thing and liberate Holy Land.

They aren't all the same in their beliefs. It was impossible to say that Crusades members were united in one belief. They may have all shared the same goals but their motivations were varied. Raymond of Toulouse had a strong faith and

Bohemond was driven by the chance of owning land for a good cause.

Just like we can't say the Crusaders weren't motivated primarily by their hatred for Muslims, we cannot say that they were motivated only by their love and loyalty to their country. Soldier life was hard, but some soldiers found it the only way to survive. While the actions of some people may be indicative of a greater need for profit, there were still many noble and valiant acts that were committed during Crusades.

Poor behavior will prevail wherever there is men. There will be tragedy where soldiers are present. The cause of war is not important; violence and brute force are the nature of warfare. It's absurd to suggest that Crusaders could have been more behaved for their religious beliefs. Many of their crimes were against humanity.

Myth 3 – The Crusades Were a Religious War

While the Crusades had many motivations, the ultimate goal was to defeat another religion. The First Crusades goals were to liberate Holy Land, and stop the Seljuk Turks creating a hole in Byzantine Empire. Because they were from another religion, it was justifiable that the Pope called for an attack.

As we'll see from the other Crusades, there were many motives behind the Crusades. They were mostly political. The Catholic Church in that time was struggling with maintaining unity amongst its members, including those who were schisming to different branches of Christianity and others who were simply fighting one another.

The idea that Crusades were needed to bring down another religion is too simplistic. It doesn't take into consideration the fact that most Crusaders went home after the primary objective had been achieved. The Pope has never called to destroy another religion, especially Islam.

The Islamic armies were also not interested in waging war against Christianity. While some of the Seljuk Turks did fight to take control over mainly Christian realms, it was because they were motivated primarily by expanding their force and size. At that time, the Islamic Forces of Asia Minor were busy fighting within themselves for control much like the Christian force in Europe. Even after the first Crusade ended, the Fatimid Caliphate refused to engage with European Crusaders. But, it did respond to protect its own territory. Territory taken from the Seljuk Turks

Myth 4; The Crusades were different from other Wars

This myth is a reminder of the fact that the Crusades had as their primary purpose to wage holy war. It's not true that religion, war and new warfare combined to create something completely different is all it seems. The Crusades are no different than any other series of military conflicts among those who want to seize land or repel their enemies. Every war has a basic theme: everyone wants something. Violence is the only way they will settle it. The Crusades had one goal: to secure Jerusalem from Muslims. This doesn't make war any special. The Crusades were unique in terms of their faith aspect, the language, and the adornment. But the crusades' core purpose was very similar to thousands other wars.

The Crusades are a core myth that explains why the Crusades were so evil. One of most commonly repeated claims is that Crusades resulted from religion. This argument is absurd, as it fails to take into account the fact that in Europe's historical past, conflicts over territory, control, or the desire to plunder were very common. The Crusades had a religious component, there is no question about that. Although the Papacy was able to mobilize its population to war with its powerful position, it is no different from any other government.

The Crusades were not about hatred of other faiths or the Christian's desire for purge those not believing the same, but rather about securing a set of military goals. While historical revisionism has unfortunately made the Crusades appear to be out of context, they were actually a fancy name that refers to wars that have always occurred during that time.

Let's take this into consideration and let's move onto the next Crusade.

Chapter 5: The Second Crusade

The time span between the first and third crusade lasted approximately forty-eightyears. The political climate in Europe was changing. And with it, the rumblings and wars started again. For the context of the Second Crusade let's take a look at one of the weakest Crusader states to see how it was a crucial part of the revival and success of Holy War.

The County Edessa is one of the Crusader state that was founded in the First Crusade. The county faced numerous attacks from many enemies, including the Seljuk Turks. Edessa was located close to these lands making it an easy target. Thus, it was constantly under threat and siege by Muslim opposition.

Imad ad-Din Zengi was a Turkish leader whose force was expanding and gaining territory while he attempted to take control over Damascus. Damascus was allied to the Kingdom in Jerusalem at that time. Zengi's forces were also working with them. Edessa's allies were killed, and the country was weaker than ever.

King Fulk from Jerusalem was among the dead. It left Edessa in a weak state after the loss of a valuable ally. Jocelyne, the leader of Edessa had been involved in a military campaign with one of his allies to seize Aleppo. Jocelyne was able to rally his forces, leading them towards Aleppo. His city was left open. Jocelyne wouldn't have known Zengi, an extreme opportunist. He would regret leaving his city.

Zengi quickly mobilizes his troops and reaches Edessa. However, he discovers that there is no army within the city. Zengi was successful in breaking through Edessa's walls using both wall-mining methods and siege weaponry. His forces then ran wild inside the city, killing thousands. Zengi was able to establish his own government in the city and take it as his. After seizing several more territories, Zengi returned to Mosul to take his place.

Jocelyne tried everything he could to retain control of the territories that weren't yet seized. Zengi was assassinated in 1146 by a rival, but Jocelyne wasn't strong enough to be able to retain the territory. Zengi was quick to expel him. Edessa had been defeated and would never be again under the control Crusaders.

Eugene III the Pope, who was in Europe at the moment, heard about Edessa's fall and decided to issue a formal declaration calling for a reaction to the loss. A papal bull was a special kind a charter that is only issued by a Pope. It called for a Second Crusade. The Bull requested King Louis VII, France, and his subjects to take up arms against the Islamic forces and lead a Crusade that would retake Edessa.

For those who were willing to take up arms and serve this Crusade faithfully, there was a promise of indulgences as well as absolutes. This Crusade would be much more organized than that of the first. Pope Eugene directed Eugene's charge at the King Of France so that he could organize forces that would have a central and well-managed structure, in contrast to the First Crusade.

Louis VII, also called Louis the Young and King of France, originally planned for military action against the Holy Land. Some historians believe the King was planning his own military action, while others suggest that he was interested only in a pilgrimage. He became excited when he heard of the Crusade. His goals were similar to those of the Pope.

Saint Bernard Clairvaux was given the responsibility of spreading the message on the Crusades. Saint Bernard of Clairvaux was tasked with spreading the message of the Crusades. Bernard preached the powerful message of forgiveness and freedom that moved hearts. He also promised the Pope's blessing if the men took up arms and served the Pope. Commoner and royalty both responded to his appeal and soon, forces rose up from every corner to defend the Pope's threat.

Bernard made the same journey to Germany where a separate Crusade emerged, known as "The Wendish Crusade". This was also authorized by the Pope who had promised similar rewards for those who served in either the French or German campaigns. Wendish Crusade - which we'll be looking at in a bit more detail - was primarily aimed towards the Polobian Slavs. Also known as Wends, they were pagans who threatened to overthrow the Holy Roman Empire.

As both French & Germanic forces prepared to lead their troops to victory against Muslim forces, the drums of battle were pounding. The Great Seljuk Empire held most of the Crusader territories. At that time the armies of states were usually made up of Turk Mamluks. These skilled professional soldiers, who were sold like slaves, had the freedom to bear arms and follow their masters in the art of war. The Mamluk was an equivalent of a knight in Europe, both in terms skill and armaments.

The Second Crusade did not have the same success as the First Crusade. It had more royalties and appeared more organized. After King Louis VII (France) and King Conrad III (Germany), the papacy fell to the sidelines. The Pope had divinely directed the war but it would be led by rulers rather than the Church. Echoing the First Crusade and the First Crusade both armies went to Constantinople to meet and plan to liberate Edessa.

Conrad III, who had heard the sermon of Saint Bernard, was intrigued by the Holy War. He joined the cause with great enthusiasm and rallied his soldiers to take his force of 20,000 troops towards Byzantine. There he would meet his French counterparts in Constantinople.

The Byzantines were not thrilled to see a large force 20,000 Germans suddenly arrive on their territory. Manuel I Komnenos the Emperor of the time was concerned about the possibility that these forces had plans for conquest. Conrad and Byzantines reacted to this situation by clashing at Constantinople. Conrad remained in control of the situation until he decided that it would be best to move into Asia Minor.

This decision to advance deeper into enemy territory wasn't a wise one. Conrad decided that without French forces, he would split his troops into two different groups and march them toward two strategic points. Conrad's first group would move towards Antonalia led by Conrad. Otto Freising (half-brother to Conrad) would lead the second armies along the coast.

Conrad's army felt thirsty due to the depleting supplies of water. They found a small, quiet river to lay down and take a rest. They were not far from Dorylaeum. This was a Turkish city.

Conrad didn't know how exposed his forces had been until they were struck from all angles by the Turkish soldiers who took the opportunity attack and destroy their Germanic foe. Conrad's force was outnumbered. Conrad issued a retreat and fled to Nicaea. His forces were defeated, while those who didn't get killed or fled were sold into slavery.

Conrad returned from Nicaea feeling miserable and with very few soldiers left. He was required to be present and in command because he was a monarch. However, the Crusade had ended, and the Germans were no longer the major players. He would continue to follow the example of his allies. However, it was going to be the French that were in charge at this point.

Things weren't much better for Otto Freising as well as the Germans traveling along the coast. They were attacked by Turkish troops and killed immediately. The few survivors were forced to flee or enslaved. Otto was able escape, but these forces were mainly non-combatants. They weren't fit to fight against the Seljuks.

This military failure would be the foundation of the Second Crusade. Things did not go according to plan.

Although the reception of the French in Constantinople was better than that of the Germans it was still met with suspicion. Most of the territory taken during the First Crusade by the Crusaders was theirs, and not the Byzantine Empire. Emperor Manuel wondered if the Crusaders really intended to be noble.

Emperor Manuel had reached an agreement with the Seljuk State of Rum to end hostilities. This was to enable his nation consolidate its power, and to prepare themselves for fighting the Crusading force that was passing through. Manuel's designs weren't always aggressive but he was not going to allow his nation to be ravaged and destroyed once again by Crusaders.

The Byzantine empire would not support the French forces, despite the exchange being amicable. No troops would be sent, unlike the previous Crusade, when Emperor Alexius was the main supporter of the war effort. The combination of the lack of faith that the Crusaders would succeed and tensions from the German forces that had already passed through the region agitated some French troops, who were outraged at Emperor Manuel's making peace with their adversaries. Some even called out for an invasion of Constantinople. Louis VII, however settled his nerves and pledged his loyalty to Manuel.

King Louis VII embarked with his troops on a journey towards Asia Minor, not knowing the serious threats he would encounter. Conrad and his 2,000-strong remaining forces eventually managed to be reunited with King Louis VII, who continued his march toward Laodicea in January 1148. Louis was soon confronted by Turkish troops who kept his forces under siege and engaged in quick skirmishes in order to weaken the Crusading armies.

In a schism that caused serious damage, the Crusaders set up camp in the mountains. However, Geoffrey Poitou, the commander of the forces responsible, decided to move the troops into a valley. After arriving at the campsite, they were unable to locate their forces that had been responsible to prepare the site and protect their flanks.

These foolishnesses were exploited by the Turks who quickly attacked the Crusaders using speed and brutality. The attacks eventually defeated them. King Louis is said even to have climbed onto a rock or a branch in an effort to hide from the attackers. Although the enemy stopped following them when night fell, the Crusaders had already taken a beating.

Geoffrey from Poitou (one of the Queen's men) was disgraced and told to return home. The forces marched through the mountains to Attalia.

Crusaders suffered another division. King Louis VII decided to go by sea, as he was fed up of the hassles of travelling by land. He organized his forces in the city and directed the governor to supply him with a fleet. However the ships provided weren't sufficient to host an entire army. Many ships had either been damaged or were unable reach the city due to recent storms. Louis chose to pack up his ships with as many troops and crew as he could, and then set sail. His remaining forces would march to Antioch.

After their king's departure, the Lords took charge. These knights and lords decided to travel by sea. However, they had to wait for available ships before setting sail for Antioch. The Crusade's foot and other soldiers were left to their own devices, with no leader.

The constant Turks attacks and the governor who just wanted them all to leave the city because of the attention they were getting, forced the Crusaders into leaving and making their way to Antioch via foot. These forces would come under severe attack repeatedly, and only half would reach Antioch.

Louis had to confront more than military obstacles upon reaching Antioch. Raymond of Toulouse was welcomed by King Louis. The Queen's Uncle pressed Louis to join Raymond during the war effort against Aleppo. If Aleppo could be defeated, Edessa's siege on would be much less difficult and the Crusaders goal would be achieved.

The decision came under pressure from all sides. Raymond, French nobility, even the Queen, all strongly supported the decision to attack Aleppo. Louis however was concerned about the political objectives of the Crusade. He was a religious, and he had initially chosen to embark on this Crusade in order to make a pilgrimage into the Holy Land. He stated that he did not wish to empower any other power politically, and that his forces would not strike at Aleppo and liberate Edessa. He said instead that they would head to Jerusalem.

This was not appreciated. This logic was hard to comprehend, since that wasn't the entire point of Crusades to free Edessa. The Queen was against any plan to move to Jerusalem. She tried to convince the King to fight at Aleppo. Louis and his wives were in great tension after rumors about her began to surface. There had been rumors about the Queen having an affair. Raymond of Toulouse wasn't that much older than Louis. They spent an inordinate amount time together. Louis was made suspicious by the fact that she was advocating for Louis' uncle's cause and even threatening her to stay behind and think about divorce.

But the King wasn't afraid to leave for Jerusalem. His wife requested that he leave, but he didn't hesitate to send her along. Louis had her arrested and ordered him to move his entire army out of Antioch over night.

Louis quickly made his way to Jerusalem and joined the Council of Acre. The Council of Acre was a large convention that focused on the Crusaders goals and came up with a plan of attack. Many rulers, lords, and nobles were present at the Council of Acre. They had many different ideas.

Crusaders arrived in Jerusalem to welcome them. There was a strong enemy in Damascus. Other Crusaders had other goals, including plundering or personal power. They also sought to target other people. King Baldwin, looking to build a stronger political presence in Jerusalem, called for Damascus' strength as well as its numbers. If the city is taken, it will be a serious blow to Muslim forces in the area and would help strengthen the cause for the Crusades.

Edessa (the inciting incident and the reason for the Crusades) was not even discussed. Damascus was chosen as a target by most people. Jerusalem was perceived as a grave threat and it was seen by most as a prime opportunity to fight. The Crusaders decided to fight Damascus.

Mu'in ad-Din Unur at the time was Damascus' ruler. He had been known to support Jerusalem against his own enemies, Zengi. However, even at Council of Acre, he was legally at peace with Jerusalem. King Baldwin sought to empower himself because he was young and struggling to get his family's legitimacy. A major city like Damascus would help him consolidate his power, and give him more authority. Mu'in knew that and had begun fortifying and raising troops in Damascus as soon the Crusaders pressed towards Jerusalem.

Final decision by the Crusaders: They would continue to Siege Damascus.

Chapter 6: The Siege of Damascus (and Lisbon)

The Crusaders made their way to Damascus on July 23rd in 1148. There was a large amount of orchards along this side of Damascus which allowed the Crusaders easily to keep fed as they marched towards the city. The city had already raised a cry of help and was soon answered.

It is generally agreed that the Crusade's decision to attack Damascus, while not the best, was the single most significant moment of the Second Crusade. The Crusaders were forced to retreat after the Crusaders received reinforcements.

Crusaders were forced off the walls and began moving towards the eastern city. The location was without water or fortifications.

Fighting was fierce on both ends, but Crusaders just didn't possess the organization, numbers or position to fight back. They had allowed themselves be surrounded by enemy soldiers, and would eventually have to retreat.

The entire siege took place over four days. The Crusaders attacked the walls in a promising manner, building siege engines with wood from Orchards. However, reinforcements arrived quickly and the craftiness displayed by Damascus residents led to their rapid repulse. Even those who had been calling to attack Damascus decided to flee. Therefore, they marched all the route back to Jerusalem, with Turkish arches following their trail, harassing them.

The Siege of Damascus resulted in a defeat and the term used to describe it is "Fiasco". This was essentially the end of Second Crusade. The Princes, nobles, and the kings returned to Jerusalem with deep distrust. Many blamed their fellows for the failure. There was also a deep shame over the loss. For such a vast undertaking and journey, it was necessary for armies and convoys to be raised across Europe into Asia Minor. Furthermore, it was necessary for a large number of peers to get together to plan for an attack. Unfortunately, the Crusade leadership couldn't bear to see the end of this four-day siege.

Many fled right away and went home immediately after the failure. Louis stayed for some time, to celebrate Easter with his family and help in fighting. But after that defeat, every Crusader who rolled into Palestine with a goal of fighting the Turks was gone. The Second Crusade originally called for Edessa liberation, but it was a complete failure that would ruin the records of the crusades for nearly 40 years.

Despite its supposed organization and circumstances, it did very little to affect the Crusader power changes. This war was a defeat and a embarrassing blemish on the church's history. The Crusades caused turmoil in the East by inciting conflict amongst local powers. These powers had previously been working alongside the crusaders. This would ultimately cause Damascus to be on hostile terms and not even safe terms.

Before we proceed to the Third Crusade. Let's begin with the Wendish Crusade.

Saint Bernard was visiting Germany to tell about the Crusade. He also called for the Holy Call to Arms to free Edessa. There was a religious frenzy amongst the faithful Christians in Germany. But not all of these individuals wanted to go to war with

Muslims. They were instead arguing passionately about the justifications for going after the Wends, pagans.

The Wends were tribal polytheists and worshipped nature. The Wends were friendly towards outsiders, however they were hostile to missionaries. They often drove out or killed those who tried to spread their faith to Wendish lands.

Despite the assertions that the Wends were fighting to convert to Christianity, it was likely that their true goal was to seize the land they held. But they were so convinced that Saint Bernard contacted Saint Bernard who extended the call for Crusade to Wendish. He also stated that all spiritual advantages from liberating Edessa to those who sought resistance to the supposed encroachment of the heathen Wends would also apply.

The Saxons, Danes, and others saw this as a justification to start war against the Wends. Prior to this invasion, Adolph II, Count, had been trying to establish a healthy and solid relationship with the Wends. Adolph II hoped to get both Germans to work side-by-side. This led to tribes being attacked by Christians who feared they would lose control of their lives if Christian influence continued. The Crusade was then made visible.

When the Crusade was announced, Prince Nyklot became a pagan prince and invaded the land Count Adolph. He seized Wagaria. The combined forces led by the Danes Saxons, Poles and Poles struck quickly. Henry the Lion and Saxony led the assault against Nyklot's Dobin fortress.

The Danes had tried fighting in the Wendish land but were continuously harassed from Nyklot's forces who constantly intercepted their vessels and attacked them on foot. As they suffered defeat after failure, the rival leaders from Denmark became increasingly heated and began to blame each other. They eventually gave up on the Crusade, and moved to the warfront.

Nyklot was ultimately defeated by Henry the Lion's siege on Dobin. However, Nyklot held a fort strategically superior to his position but he didn't have enough food and water to sustain a long-term siege. The Wends eventually surrendered the city and converted to Christianity.

Albert the Bear had led the other armies to Stettin in a march to capture the Christian city. They were planning to seize the city, but the leaders of the town tried to explain it to Albert and the rest of his army. The Saxons seemed to not care at all and tried to persuade the city to be seized, but the religious leaders convinced them that they should just give up. The Saxon soldiers, disillusioned with their loss of potential profit, fled the area.

The Wendish Crusade consisted essentially of a failed attempt to convert pagans. Any such conversions that were made under the threat death was merely lip service. The pagans then simply returned to what they believed to be after scrutiny had been lifted.

Henry the Lion kept his campaign for warfare going, looking for profit and plunder. He did not push the Wends to convert. Over this time, territories changed rapidly and conversions became merely lip service.

The Wendish Crusades, although justified by Pope Benedict XVI, were nothing more than territorial opportunism executed by greedy and land-mongering force who all wanted to expand under their assumed faith banner.

Despite all the confusion and gross incompetence that accompanied the Second Crusade there was one decisive victory where the Crusaders played a part, although it is still unclear whether the Siege in Lisbon was actually part the Crusades.

Spain attempted to take control of Moors during the Middle Ages. Spain tried to do the same for control of Iberian Peninsula. This conflict was ongoing for a very long time. The Crusades were not over yet. This time period is known as "The Reconquista" or the Reconquest.

King Alfonso VII was from Leone and Castile. He was involved in fighting the Moors. Moors are Spanish Muslims who have been at war for nearly 100 years with the Portuguese. After declaring Second

Crusade, the Pope spoke favorablely about the conflict that existed between the Moors of Spain and the Iberian Peninsula. He also claimed it to be part of the Crusade. The Flemish Normans English, Scottish Crusaders were collectively called the Franks. Their mobilization to move towards Holy Land was hampered by severe weather and they landed on the Iberian Shore.

Alfonso did not look like a gift horse and demanded a meeting. He also made his case against the Moors for seizing Lisbon. The cause of Spaniards did not appeal to the Franks. They were more interested to move against the Muslims of Syria to protect the Holy Land and not get caught in any long drawn out war between the Spanish Moors. It took some negotiations and promises of all of the city's spoils but eventually, the Crusaders agreed on a side with Alfonso to support him in his goal of capturing Lisbon. They would organize to fight against Lisbon and then hopefully return to Jerusalem.

Alfonso ordered Alfonso's capture of the city, armed with his newly acquired armoury. Soon the Christian forces were leading a siege to Lisbon. After four months of siege, finally the city surrendered. It was agreed that Muslims would be protected from danger. The Crusaders captured control of the city. This was the only significant victory recorded during the Second Crusade.

It is interesting to mention that there is general disagreement over whether this was a Crusade part or if it was part o the Reconquista. Although the fighting took places outside of Levant the Pope allowed the Crusaders to continue their actions. He had already approved of the invasion of Lisbon. It's clear that this action was part and parcel of the Second Crusade.

Chapter 7: The King's Crusade

The First Crusade, which was a success; the Second Crusade, which was an utter disaster and embarrassed everyone involved, was not the same as the Third Crusade. The Third Crusade or the King's Crusade is a far more complex threat that required a much greater response.

Nur ad-Din (the Emirate at Damascus), had been steadily growing power and unifying Syria. He took initiative and became the ruler a unified Islamic State. It was this that he began to be bolder against the Crusaders who supported him in fighting. His reign as Syria's most powerful leader was secured after an attack on Antioch. He died of a fever in 1174.

Nu ad–Din's 11-year-old boy inherited the throne. But, the truth is that he was not positioned to lead an army against the Crusaders as well as work to unify Syria or Egypt. With the power vacuum, a man later to be called Saladin rose up and assumed the position of vassal for Nur ad-Din's young son. All the while pursuing his political ambitions.

Saladin gained control over the Syrian, Egyptian and Libyan forces in no time. He was also crowned the Sultans of Egypt and Syria after a long and successful military campaign. His relations with Crusaders were suspicious, since he was trying to expand Syria's territory by acquiring control over several Crusader countries.

The military forces from Saladin clashed with Jerusalem several times. In the end, an all-out siege was imposed on Jerusalem in 1187. This was a bloody and violent battle. However, it became evident that Jerusalem was not capable of defending itself against the attackers. Therefore, they offered Saladin some peace. Saladin quickly agreed and took control. Saladin treated all residents of the city with respect. He also allowed those who paid a ransom to be freed, as well elderly and infirm people. Saladin said that he wouldn't be destroying the Church of the Holy Sepulcher.

Saladin continued to hold territory from Crusader states and took control over Acre. Gregory VII, the current Pope heard about this information and issued an official bull calling for a Third Crusade. The Pope said that the sins and power of the people had led the to the recapture and rise of Saladin. He urged the world to stop the tide from turning the tide with Crusading. There weren't stated goals in bull. However, it was widely believed that crusade would secure Jerusalem once again.

Different from the Crusades II and III, the Saladin Tithe, or tithe, was introduced. It was created in France as well as England. This tithe (or tax) would be used for funding the Crusaders' war effort. It was important to note that those who joined the Crusade were exempted from tax, and this was a significant incentive for them to participate in the war.

France and England had been at war. But when the Crusade news came out, their feud ended. Henry II, King England, died before Crusade, leaving Richard, the Lionheart, in command of his kingdom. Phillip the I. France, Henry II's ally, agreed that he would also go on a holy campaign. Thus, the two kings began preparing to wage war against Saladin.

Frederick I Barbarossa was the Emperor and Head of the Holy Roman Empire. He heard the Pope calling for this war. With great enthusiasm, he immediately mobilized his troops and led them toward the Holy Land. He had a large army with him. Little did he know, the Byzantines had secretly agreed to undermine Frederick's movements as a condition of peace. Saladin was very close to the Byzantine Empire making them vulnerable.

Frederick Barbarossa didn't make it to Antioch. However, his horse was struck by a rock while crossing a creek and his horse fell, throwing Frederick against the rocks. He suffered injuries and ended up drowning in the river. With the sudden death their emperor, the overwhelming majority of Germans returned home. Frederick Barbarossa's horse fell and threw Frederick against the rocks, injuring him. Frederick's only son, however, continued onwards to Antioch. Their forces were modest, at most 5,000 men.

Phillip and Richard both fled the battlefield to confront the threat. They met briefly in Sicily. A dispute over marital rights broke out and they parted ways. Richard went to Cyprus to conquer it, while Phillip headed to Tyre. It was in Tyre where the Third Crusade's most important battles began.

Conrad of Montferrat, the so called King of Jerusalem, began the Siege of Acre, which is widely considered one of the most fatal battles of the Crusades. Conrad, Guy of Lusignan's husband, had made it his mission to become King of Jerusalem. Guy and Conrad fought for control over a Kingdom that was swiftly captured by Saladin. Guy had been held hostage by Saladin and was eventually released as a means to reach an agreement with Tyre.

Conrad refused Guy the authority of King and refused to allow Guy to enter Tyre. Guy, who was trying for the victory against Saladin, was faced with this problem. Guy eventually managed to reach an agreement with some powers, William II from Sicily and the Archbishopof Pisa. These gave Guy sufficient force to take Acre as his base of operations.

Philip, on the other hand, had sided with Conrad, and supported him in his decision for Jerusalem to be the throne. He agreed to support Tyre's siege of Acre and to help Guy, independently of Guy. The goal of the mission was to force Saladin back, and to gain a stronger foothold inside the country. Acre could certainly help with that.

Philip agreed to lead a siege, but his efforts proved futile. He assisted with the preparation of soldiers and in the building of siege weapons. However, he was more concerned in waiting for English soldiers to arrive to assist. Richard the Lionheart, upon his arrival, quickly established control over the operation and began preparing the soldiers for the forthcoming battle against Acre.

But the siege at Acre was not over until Richard and Phillip arrived. Saladin's troops were very strong, and Crusader force prepared for a direct assault on the city walls. Saladin led his troops to attack Guy's encampment. Both sides suffered significant damage. The Christian forces struggled to fight without cohesion. While the Crusaders were capable of repelling the attack, their greed seized control once Saladin began to retreat from his flanks. From that point, the Crusaders began quickly to plunder and loot, distracted only by the lucrative treasures they had. Saladin managed to regroup and lead his cavalry as a charge against scattered and distracted Crusaders.

Conrad's life ended up in peril after the counterattack. Guy, Conrad's rival, was able to save him. Although the battle was intense, even though Conrad was forced to his limits by the cavalry attack, the Crusaders held their ground and repelled the enemy advance.

The battle was fierce, but the fighting stopped. The Crusaders increased their numbers with more soldiers joining the siege. They were able then to build a formal blockade on Acre. Even though Emperor Barbarossa arrived, the news was good for both the Crusaders (and the troops and soldiers of Saladin), as he expected a large army soon to arrive. Both sides created their forces in what some call a double Siege. Saladin was attacking the Crusaders' city of Acre while the Crusaders were trying to take it.

King Richard finally arrived in June 1191. With Phillip's siege weapons and the siege lines already laid by the Crusaders the only thing left was to get the siege arms and take control of Acre.

Saladin would organize an attack to distract the Crusaders, giving Acre time to rebuild. While this went on for several times, it was evident that the Crusaders weren't large enough and that the presences of the Kings meant that organization at its best.

The siege was dragging on and finally the city tried surrendering but Richard was not pleased with the terms. Saladin's assistance and counter-attacks became less frequent and the city found itself in serious difficulties. They offered many things in a negotiations, money, and hostages as part the surrender. Finally, Saladin's command, a deal was reached. Two-hundred, thousand gold coins would be given by the Crusaders. In return, two thousand prisoners would be released. Richard accepted the deal. The year-long siege was now over. The Crusaders had their first major victory against Saladin. They also gained a substantial foothold on Syria.

King Richard waited, after his victory, for Saladin to pay him and free the prisoners.

Saladin was slow at fulfilling his obligations, releasing a few prisoners but sending very few payments. Richard wasn't happy with this. He believed Saladin was just trying to stall to get enough troops for a counterattack. Richard demanded Saladin release several key prisoners or give a list to the ransomed hostages. Saladin refused. Richard was furious and demanded Saladin's immediate return of the prisoners and all money.

Richards did not ask Saladin to respond and King Richard decided he would make a big deal of the captives he had captured while capturing Acre. Richard gathered 3000 men on Ayyadieh's hill and ordered their execution. This became known by the name "Massacre of Ayyadieh". Saladin and his forces were powerless to stop the executions. Saladin responded to Richard's cruelty by execution the Christian prisoners he kept. They exchanged barbarism and moved on. King Richard knew that there was no way to transport prisoners. But he was not someone who would give prisoners up for no reason. Saladin's actions would have weakened the agreement they had reached. King Richard decided to use this tactic to show Saladin he meant business.

Richard continued on, leading his force to Jaffa. He would then become involved in Battle of Arsuf.

King Richard, after securing Acre in the Crusade was primarily in command. Phillip had since departed France in poor health. This left the Lionheart as the commander of the operation. Richard's objective was to capture Jerusalem. This would require a strong tactical foothold of nearby ports. He then set his sights upon Jaffa, where his troops would have water and reinforcements from the boat.

The march to Jaffa was hard work due to the scorching August heat, combined with constant harassment by Saladin's archers, which made it difficult for the Crusaders. King Richard maintained tight ranks and directed his men forward with discipline, fervor, and ignored the peltings of arrows against them. Saladin had intended to cause Crusaders rank to fall due to harassment. But, they held together fiercely and forced Saladin's army to attack Richard.

The Woods of Arsuf is a forest area in Palestine that was the site of the battle. Saladin had ordered his forces to wait in readiness and was preparing to strike at Richard's soldiers. The King noticed the scout units and was careful to create a formation that would stand against all sides. He knew that Saladin's tactics would cause the soldiers into chaos. So he ordered his soldiers, who were already holding their ranks together, to ignore the harassment.

Soldiers were tightly packed together. Rear flanks had to stop walking forwards to face the enemy forces advancing from all directions. Richard begged Crusaders for an opportunity to attack them, but they waited. He knew that if they made a single mistake, Saladin's numerically stronger forces would destroy them. The Crusaders maintained their rank and refused to move, despite charges from enemy troops.

Two Hospitaller knights broke ranks, charging into the melee to defeat the enemy and rallying the entire Crusader Army to attack. Richard chose to use the sudden rank break to launch a counterattack against their enemy rather than allow chaos to ensue. The action was shocking to the enemy soldiers who were unaware it had been due to insubordination. They mistakenly thought it was part their clever strategy. The Ayyubid army suffered a severe morale blow when it suddenly changed from accepting accusations and holding firm to outright violence.

Saladin, who had brought his own host into this fight, escalated the fighting and Saladin's forces were stopped and turned around. Richard was too smart to allow his forces chase Saladin. Knowing that the Turks were known for their fallback tactics, Richard urged them to surrender and let the Turks chase the soldiers, killing them in chaos. Richard was eventually able to reorganize his forces and establish an Arsuf encampment once the enemy were defeated.

This was a significant victory of the Crusaders. It also dealt a devastating blow to Saladin. Saladin was previously seen as invincible and believed that he could defeat the Crusaders. The power and effectiveness of such a devastating attack against an army that relied solely on inducing chaos, loss of cohesion, and inducing chaos was greater than they were expecting. This helped greatly boost the morale among the Crusaders. In the end, King Richard would be regarded as an excellent leader in these conflicts.

Jaffa was quickly secured following all of this. Saladin drew back his forces, not wanting to engage in direct confrontations with the crusading troops due to nature of the attacks. Saladin's harass tactics made Richard's men resistible, and the Turks weren't able to strike back with the same degree of cleverness as they used. This kept Saladin out of a conflict.

King Richard went on, leading his forces to Ascalon, the fortress Saladin had been holding. Saladin adopted a scorched ground policy. He destroyed any base he left, and this was to stop his foes getting secure defenses. Ascalon was held by the Crusaders. They began to rebuild defenses. As they became more focused on Jerusalem their discussions grew heated about how best to strike at the core of the conflict.

After heated exchanges, the Duke and Burgundy of France, the leader among the soldiers of France, called for a direct invasion. King Richard said that the best way was to control Egypt first before moving to attack the city. The infighting grew to the point where they were forced to be split up, which weakened the overall strength. Richard was a man who believed in practicality. He knew that Jerusalem wouldn't be taken by his lesser troops and so he decided to retreat.

Saladin's forces attacked Jaffa unexpectedly, taking control of the city in a storm and killing all those who remained. Richard ordered his forces, in an attempt to recapture Jaffa, to immediately take notice of this siege.

Crusaders, who came from the water, launched an offensive against Saladin's soldiers that eventually led to the disintegration of the Ayyubids. Although the fighting was intense, Saladin's troops failed to prepare for a naval strike and were ultimately defeated. Saladin rallied and attacked his troops with violence. However the nature Richard's assault had already destroyed any chance Saladin had at using surprise to their advantage. Saladin was defeated and driven from the city.

Richard had made the decision before the attack in Jaffa to return home to England. Richard decided to return to England after his extensive campaign for the Holy Land. Richard was exposed when Phillip I of France started to move against Richard.

Richard had secured the ports and taken control of several key positions. After that, he felt he had done enough. He made plans to go home.

Saladin agreed to negotiate peace with Richard under the stress of being routed once more and his rapidly diminishing credibility as a result. Both sides agreed to a peace treaty. This ended hostilities. Ascalon would be given to Saladin. Saladin would still control Jerusalem, the Holy Land. But trade and pilgrimages for Christians were allowed under the agreement. Richard returned home after a long campaign when Saladin agreed. The Third Crusade was ended.

Chapter 8: One Crusade Is Over; Another One Begins

Many war veterans felt bitterly disappointed at the end of Third Crusade. Europe was not happy that Richard had led such victories against enemies only to decide to go home. Islamic Rule, on the other hand, became more concerned about Saladin's failures and inability against their enemy.

Richard's inability secure Jerusalem would result in a call for another Crusade. Just a few short years after the last Crusade ended in an unsatisfactory end, Pope Innocent III urged for another Crusade. Innocent called for the Crusade to organize his new reign. Innocent was just taking over the office. French and English troops were drawn down in a battle against each other. Germanic forces had been at odds with Pope Benedict XVI.

Innocent's goal, however, was to unite the people.

He issued a papal bill, in which he stated that the war against Muslims must be started. This Bull provided specifics and was the most well-organized of all the papal calls for Crusade.

The first Crusade was not as successful as the others. Both the French as well as the English didn't want to be involved in another crusade. Rather, they wanted to fight against each others. It would also have been difficult without the support from European kings to attract a force. Fulk, an evangelical preacher, called for participation in a tournament. Enough forces were raised to initiate the Fourth Crusade.

Boniface Montferrat, an Italian count, led the Crusade. He succeeded Count Thibaut, the Crusade's original leader. His strategy was very unlike the previous Crusades. These had involved large-scale mobilization of troops and marching across Palestine to capture various targets. Boniface wanted Egypt to be attacked, as it was where Muslim power had increased over the years. For this to happen, he would need transport across the sea.

Boniface requested help from Venice. He sent emissaries, hoping to gain transportation from Venetian trader to construct a fleet to carry his Crusader forces to Egypt. The Venetians were willing to build enough ships to carry the entire Crusade. So they started preparing for a year. As the Venetians worked on the project, Crusader troops grew. They were mainly composed of Frenchmen as well as those from Holy Roman Empire.

Once they had prepared their forces, they embarked on a journey to Venice to receive their warships. The Crusade was quickly unraveled at this point. The Crusaders, who had reached Venice, were forced to pay 85,000 sterling marks for the total cost of the fleet. Doge Dandolo who was the leader among the Venetians demanded that they be paid the entire amount before Crusaders could set sail.

Boniface's forces were unable to pay such fees due to financial constraints. They barely had enough to make a payment but their forces weren't large enough to make this investment. This was devastating for the Venetians that had worked hard to build this fleet. They were stuck in a position where the Doge was unable or unwilling to release them from debt. Also, he couldn't face any reputation consequences for refusing them transportations.

Zadar, a city that once belonged to Venice, was forced to secede and become independent by the protection of Hungary.

Doge Dandolo asked that the Crusaders sail for Zadar to seize the city. Enrico Dandolo was then able to take control over Zadar. The proposed payment method had one flaw. Zadar is a Catholic state that was protected under the papacy.

Pope Innocent III stressed that Crusaders could not fight against each other, but rather must confront the enemy that occupies Jerusalem. He had forbidden Christians from fighting against one other, and Zadar's request for invasion was considered a serious betrayal. Many crusaders rejected the request. But, it was clear that there was no other route to secure the fleet.

Peter of Capua who was representing the Pope at the moment made the argument that an invasion against Zadar was permissible because Jerusalem was ultimately their goal and they would have no chance to capture the city once again if the fleet wasn't available. The Pope quickly condemned the entire plan and threatened to excommunicate everyone involved in the Crusade, as well as Venice, if any such action was taken.

While the letter was being quietly retorted by the leader, he did not inform the soldiers about the crime against Christendom. Despite oppositions, their plan was clear. The group would sail to Zadar, launch an attack against it, and claim it as Doge Enrico Dandolo. This attack was the Crusaders' first on a Christian-based city. The Fourth Crusade would soon follow.

Before the siege on Zadar, Venetian leader made extensive use of his large army. He took his ships along the shore to several trade partners. He intimidated them. This significantly improved Venice's ability trade. The Crusaders arrived in Zadar with a huge fleet and quickly took the city under their control.

In a desperate effort to avoid trouble from the invaders, the city displayed banners that showed they were Catholic. However, these banners did no harm and the Crusaders took control of the city and broke through its defenses. A few leaders refused the fight, claiming it was not for them invade a Christian land. However, the rest took part in the fighting against this city.

The city that was Zadar did not last very long. Soon the Crusaders overtook the city, seizing it and forcing the citizens to flee. Although it was technically a victory, it was actually a loss for the Crusaders. When the Pope heard about such atrocities, he excommunicated them, calling them greedy & impure.

The Crusaders were not likely to be the last ones to attack a Christian community. As the siege began, Boniface was the Crusader leader. He had left Venice before Venice arrived to attack. He avoided excommunication and met with Alexios IV Angelos (the Byzantine Prince).

Alexios IV had been exiled to Byzantine in the wake of his father, Emperor from Byzantine's uprising. Alexios vowed to take his kingdom home and gave Boniface money so that he could pay the Venetians their debt. Boniface was also promised by Alexios that he would provide transportation and soldiers for the Crusade.

Because Crusaders lacked funds and troops, Boniface offered the opportunity. Boniface told Zadar the news. They had been occupying Zadar in winter.

Doge Enrico Dandolo (one of the greatest supporters) was a key supporter of the war effort against Constantinople. The Venetians had a fierce rival in trade with the Byzantines. Both were vying for trade supremacy and control of trade routes. Boniface was a clever man. He knew of the possibility that an attack against Constantinople, the seat for power for the Byzantines, would lead to a loss in trade opportunities for them. Enrico's deep-rooted hatred of Byzantines stemmed from the fact that Byzantines were guilty of many atrocious acts against Venetians. This was a perfect opportunity to take on his long-term enemies, so the Doge steadfastly advocated attacking Constantinople.

Boniface agreed to take part in the venture and after he reconnected back with the Crusades leadership from Zadar, it was clear that they all would be joining the effort together. This was another matter of contention for Pope Benedict XVI. Constantinople was a Christian state, but they also had doctrinal problems with the papacy and were part in a schism. The Pope wrote them asking them to cease attacking any Christian nation. However the Crusader knew what was coming. They would set sail for Constantinople in search of Alexios IV, who would then be made the emperor.

Once the Crusaders reached the Byzantine Empire in search of peace, they were met by a force under the command of Emperor Alexios III. A pretender had seized power in an upheaval and was leading the charge. As the Emperor was to pass the throne through inheritance, the Crusaders considered the Emperor's actions immoral and illegal. However by political sensibilities, the Crusaders were openly hostile to the idea of a violent uprising for new leadership.

Crusaders demanded of the pretender that he abdicate power and allow Alexius I and his father return to the throne. This request was ignored and the forces quickly became in conflict. The Byzantine army's unfortunate situation was that they could not maintain a large garrison. Therefore, troops had to be raised from other principalities in order to keep Constantinople under control. This meant that they had to be quick to rally forces in order to resist the rapid arrival of thousands more Crusaders.

As the battle prepared for both sides, it became apparent that Constantinople was about to fall. A force pretending to be Crusaders was also going to attack the city that once was home to Crusaders. This was a very serious political situation. The attack on Constantinople, while ultimately successful, would have a devastating impact on the country's political landscape.

With a pretender as the throne, the Byzantine armies were fully stocked and ready to go against the invaders. Crusaders needed to cross the Bosphorous Straight in order to attack the capital.

Alexius had also prepared his coast soldiers, lining them up ready to face their foes while awaiting the inevitable attack. Although a formidable chain had been constructed to block them from entering the harbor's entrance, the Venetians managed it to be destroyed, opening up the door to attacking Constantinople.

The beach forces were waiting for the attack but weren't ready for the cavalry charges. Venetian ships are designed in a way that warhorses carrying onboard can drop open a ramp. This allows horses to charge right out of their transports. This is a very powerful way for an enemy force to be broken through sheer force and surprise. The Crusader's Cavalry Charge immediately destroyed their opponents, allowing them access to the city.

The Varngians (mercenary forces comprising the Imperial Palace Guard) fought against the Frank's invasion and broke their initial siege. The Venetians however managed to use their Siege Towers to take over the Towers. This gave the Crusaders the opportunity to gain entry to the city.

The Emperor Alexius III organized his troops and prepared them for battle amid the chaos. He organized their ranks and led them to battle against the invading troops. He led them straight towards the Frankish soldiers. After losing his nerve, he ordered his troops to retreat. Despite all this, Crusaders could not gain any foothold in the city so they were driven away.

The Crusaders went out again the next morning with plans to press into the city. But, when they arrived, they found that Alexius III the supposed Emperor had fled in middle of the night, leaving behind his money and his daughter. The Greeks returned the throne immediately to Isaac II Angelus who was blinded and infirm.

Alexius was elected co-Emperor. His father's inability as a leader without his vision meant that he could not be trusted with power. Alexius had been crowned and it looked like the Crusaders would have their second major win. After receiving payment, the Crusaders settled within the city. Alexios was unable to pay the money back. An imposter had stolen money out of the treasury. Constantinople was then in a very bad situation. Alexios pushed for more money and raised taxes.

This angered the people, as well as showing weakness in leadership. Additionally, he committed a grave error when he tried to melt down various religious artifacts in an effort to extract the silver and gold they were made from. This decision was not just sacrilege. It also showed his desperate nature and weakened his reputation among the people. The Greeks weren't happy that the man would destroy artifacts for foreigners.

Alexius V negotiated with Crusaders in an attempt to win more time and maybe gain an advantage against his enemies. He wanted to be able to fight against Alexios III. The Emperor led some thousand soldiers to fight their enemy. When they returned to Constantinople, they discovered that it was in a state of chaos.

Some drunk crusaders from the town decided to attack the Mosque. This started a quarrel among the Byzantine Citizens,

Muslims and Crusaders. This quarrel got worse and worse, until the massive fire that destroyed a lot of homes and property spread rapidly across the entire district.

Alexios IV, his father, was no longer running the show. Although he tried his best, it became clear that he would be unable to pay the Crusaders all the help he had received. This increased tension caused by both sides. The Crusaders had been willing to take on a lot in order to fight for Alexios. They had not only put their lives in danger, but they had also chosen defiance to their Pope, who had the power of removing them from the church.

Alexios Dokas, a man known as Alexios, saw a chance to rebel against the current emperor. He had fought in the Crusader wars before and gained the respect and admiration from the Greeks. He quickly seized control of Alexios' throne, and threw the Emperor in prison before finally choosing to strangle him. He declared himself to have been Emperor Alexios, and the people accepted his reign.

Crusaders hated the fact their Emperor had died, but they were only concerned about getting paid. The Crusaders were fed up with their need for money and demanded Alexios VII pay the debt. The new Emperor, an anti-Crusader man who had gained popularity, turned down their demands and chose instead to build the city's defenses. Crusaders furious at this decision decided that they would be paid their dues, and banded together for an assault on Constantinople. They were not going be installing a new Emperor. Instead, they would be seizing it for their own use.

The Crusaders found no reason to stop them from invading this city and decided to forcefully take what was owed. This was a legitimate decision as Crusade's funding was inadequate and they couldn't pay Venetians what they owed for the fleets. While there were some who believed it would be a disgrace to God and man to go to war against the city's inhabitants, the majority agreed with this decision. Constantinople was declared to be destroyed.

The city had extremely strong fortifications. They used catapults on the Crusaders to take out the siege engines. After being in chaos for months, Alexios V wasn't able to create a response to the Crusaders.

With Venetian support, the Franks were in a position to lift a few of their soldiers through the walls. Once inside, they began to weaken the walls by ripping holes in them, allowing the Crusaders into the city. This allowed the crusading armies to gain entry to the city, and captured a part of it before accidentally setting it on fire.

This pressure proved to be too much to the new Emperor. He decided to flee chaos and regroup at Alexios' III, the imposter.

The Siege failed to last long after the loss of leadership. Soon, the Crusading Forces took control of the city.

After the city's security was achieved, looting began. There were thousands of crusaders who spent their time pillaging and stealing. There was a lot of violence in that period, with the Crusaders not paying any attention to oaths nor sacred items as they desecrated churches, looted home, destroyed works and killed many civilians. Some historians consider Constantinople's sacking to be one of humanity's worst crimes. This was the time when the once prosperous, powerful seat the Byzantine Emperor was brought down to its knees.

Both the Crusaders, Emperor, and Venetians owed enough money that the city was looted to make ends meet. They didn't intend to leave Constantinople even after the siege. Instead, a Treaty was negotiated between the Crusaders of Constantinople and the Venetians. It divided territory and created an entirely new state. Baldwin of Flanders became the Emperor of Constantinople after the Latin Empire in Constantinople was established.

This victory effectively ended Crusades. With the capture and looting the city, there was no reason for them to continue. The Pope found these actions to be inexcusable. He condemned the Crusades and ended up deeply regretting that any of them were allowed to embark on the Crusade.

The Fourth Crusade was a devastating event. Byzantine Empire had been effectively defeated by such actions. While remnants were left and the Greeks still remained in the area but they lost any majority power. Byzantines not being in power meant that Islamic States that were their neighbours would have a better position to launch wars against the West. As the Byzantines had frequently acted as a buffer keeping them back, that was the implication.

This was the end more or less of the Fourth Crusade. Although a few men were able to travel to the Holy Land without the required numbers or force, it was only a small pilgrimage. The fall of Constantinople would reverberate in history. The Latin Empire soon found itself in a battleground with enemies on all sides. This Crusade also saw a shift in political effectiveness for the Crusades.

The fact that the Papacy had lost control of the entire Crusade was a huge blow to the faith of the Church in the Crusades. Even in the face of such a disaster, the Pope was still determined to free Jerusalem. The Fifth Crusade, which would take place not too long after Constantinople's fall, would soon be launched.

Chapter 9: The Fifth Crusade

Despite the failures in the Fourth Crusade, Pope Innocent III was determined to liberate Holy Land. He continued to preach for Crusade, attempting to unite a force powerful enough and disciplined to take Jerusalem away from the Islamic forces.

Innocent issued two more papal bulls, one 1208 and one 1215, calling again for a Crusade. He called a Fourth Council of Lateran together, which he called for the raising of force. With this, he was able enough to motivate a force to rally around him. Innocent's plan was to mobilize the forces and to direct them, allowing that the Papacy could run the war effort like in the First Crusade. This would prevent something similar to what happened with the Fourth Crusade.

Innocent died in order to be able continue the war effort. Innocent was replaced by Honorius III. Honorious believed the power of Crusade too and continued the church's policy in recovery of Jerusalem.

King Andrew II (Hungary) was one of the first people to take the Crusade vow. He also raised his forces to join the crusade against the infidels. He got his troops together and set out for Acre with John of Brienne to meet the King of Jerusalem.

After all the leadership met at Acre, the war council was immediately established. Then began a long discussion on how to get Jerusalem under control. Egypt was primarily viewed in this way as the largest source of power for the prevailing Muslim authorities in the land. Cairo, the home to Al-Kamil would be easy to capture. This was considered a good plan, so a campaign started to establish an Egyptian siege.

The city near the Nile Delta was the first target. Capturing Damietta could give the

Crusaders enough strength to move on Cairo and unseat Sultan. The plan was for ships to be used to travel up the river, to capture Damietta and then continue to travel through the river towards Cairo.

Along with their plan to attack the city, Crusaders made Keykavus II, an unlikely ally. Keykavus was a Sultan that saw the Ayyubids in the same light. Keykavus was able to handle Syria, so the Crusaders didn't have to worry too much about fighting on two separate fronts.

The Crusaders entered Damietta in July. Despite their actions they were unable to take over all of the towers but not the city. Al-Kamil's plans for defending the city were more focused on defense than on attacking because the waterways were too well defended. They had tried to attack the Crusaders, but they were too strong. Instead of retreating from the city, they focused on protecting Damietta and keeping it fortified.

Al-Kamil tried to bargain with them for peace, but their requests were not heard. The worst part about the situation was that Al-Kamil had actually offered Jerusalem to be traded for Damietta. Cardinal Pelagius (Crusader Leader at the Time) declined. This was probably due to Jerusalem's Wall being destroyed by Ayyubids in an attempt to prevent Christian forces, if ever captured, from defending the city.

But, the Crusade was primarily about saving Holy Land. There was some contention over this. Some men, including William I (Count of Holland), left the military upon this decision.

The siege continued. However, it took several months for Damietta to be defeated and the port town was captured.

John of Brienne was the representative for the Pope and Pelagius were at odds over who owned the city. John argued for Pelagius' claim that the city should be held by the Papacy since it was the Church that organized the Crusade. John argued, however that the city belonged only to John as the rightful ruler over Jerusalem. John finally took his forces and returned home to Acre. This caused a dispute between them.

Pelagius waited some time to see if more reinforcements would be sent, but these reinforcements never arrived. This placed the Crusaders at risk of losing their troops, which put them in danger of abandoning their plans to march upon Cairo. Al-Kamil was busy taking care of various insurrections. Keykavus was also vying for Al-Kamil's attention.

Pelagius did not serve as a wartime Commander. He was the representative the Pope. This holy man was responsible for looking after the spiritual needs and the camp. However the Church had wanted to give him the leadership power in order to run the war. He was not a military strategist so he waited for additional forces to arrive. Al-Kamil's waiting would end up costing the Crusaders much in terms of opportunity. He had built his troops in the winter and was quickly in a position of power again.

John of Brienne was eventually able to regain control over the Crusade. They marched out to Cairo in an attempt to capture the city. Their forces were quickly assembled and they marched across the desert to face their enemy. The Ayyubids started a campaign of harassment against the troops, picking at them and moving in and around with raiding maneuvers to weaken the morale.

Crusaders tried to cross a dry channel to reach the Nile. However, the Nile had flooded immediately, and they were unable to continue their plans. This resulted in a crisis. The Crusaders were carrying relatively few supplies due to the hope of being able quickly to capture a few Fortifications and secure supplies.

Pelagius was shocked to discover that their only strategy to cross the Nile had failed. He ordered a retreat and commanded the soldiers to make their way back through the channel from which they had come. Their surprise was that the channel had flooded too, leaving them in an extremely vulnerable position. They were cut off on both sides and found themselves in a difficult spot. Ayyubid took full advantage, and brought his troops to attack the Crusaders during the night. It caused an enormous number of casualties. King John led the counter attack, working to save his soldiers but the damage had already been done.

Al-Kamil had always been determined to find peace, even from the beginning of the war effort. He had tried many times to reach an agreement, but Pelagius rejected him. However, at this point of Fifth Crusade they knew that they had no chance of victory. Pelagius gave up control of Damietta to get their freedom. He also signed an agreement for peace, agreeing to not wage war on each other for eighteen year. With this agreement, the Fifth Crusade came to an end without any major victory.

Inept leadership in allowing a Church figure to lead the war decision making was one reason this Crusade was a failure. While the Papacy was aware of the danger of seeing yet another Crusade fail in its attempt to attack Christendom, it had also been concerned that the Pope would give

Pelagius more authority than he should when it came time for decision making. Pelagius could have fought against Cairo and taken control of Jerusalem if he had more military knowledge. This Crusade, however, failed again.

This Crusade was essentially what the Papacy called the last major Crusade. The incompetence and sheer loss of life that were evident during these military campaigns was too much to bear. Therefore, it was not possible to call for the liberation Jerusalem. The Crusades lasted, but they were not under the control of the Church. Instead, many of them were led individually by countries who wanted the Holy Land to be liberated and financed their armies.

The Sixth Crusade of Frederick II of Holy Roman Empire, which was one such Crusade that proved to be one of the most popular in history, was perhaps one of the most important Crusades.

The Crusades as well as the Birth of Knighthood

"You are called shepherds. Do not act like hiredlings. Your crooks should always be in your hands, but you must be true shepherds. Guard the flock and do not let it go. The gospel tells us that you are the salt to the earth. However, if you do not fulfill your obligation, how is it possible to make it saluable?" - Pope Urban II

The silky sea sand dunes seems like it stretches endlessly. The golden grains appear almost gold under the midday sunlight. As a wind gust blows by, a swirling pattern of sand moves delicately through the open space. The scenery would be stunning if not the swarms of black figures looming from the distance, which are steadily increasing in size. The thunderous hooves of over a thousand horses and the iron-clad men on top of them, holding their weapons or shields, make the ground shake. Even distantly, the thunderous cries of their iron-clad men roar across the open air, their words as clear and loud as ever: "Kill every infidel!"

Charging from a different side is also a powerful sight. A multitude of men dressed in sparkling armor lean forward holding their reins tightly between their fists. Quilted coverings draped behind them are the result. There are many men in turbans with conical helmets who wield bows andarrows, spears, or mighty swords alongside them.

This is the most common response to the crusades.

First of all, a crusade was a holy battle, but they were only allowed to be classified as such by Pope Francis. These papal-approved military operations were intended to eliminate the enemies of Christ and "infidels" in Islam. It may seem as though the Catholics are only concerned with forced conversions and taking over churches, but there was much more under the hood.

After centuries spent under persecution, Christianity was made the official religion for the Roman Empire. Constantine I the Great, who led the eastern half the Empire, established Jerusalem and Levant as the capital of the Empire. This area also controlled the flow and movement of pilgrims. However, the Byzantines collapsed and were replaced by an "Abrahamic", a third religion from the Arabian Peninsula called Islam. Jerusalem was seized by the Arab Muslim Army in 634 A.D. Christians were devastated and unable to recover it for several centuries.

This loss was compounded by disagreements regarding the pilgrimage rights to Jerusalem, for Jews as well as Christians. There was a lot of uncertainty over access to holy places for Christians and Muslims, as the Muslim rulers had varied their views on tolerance of different religious groups. This made it difficult to maintain a Christian or Jewish identity. While it remains unclear whether the Levant was tolerant of Muslims at the time, there is no doubt that the Christians were anxious about losing control of holy sites. Political instability was also caused by continued expansion and contraction along the Byzantine Empire's borders.

However, the Arab Muslims also lost control over Levant to a new group that came from West Asia through Persia. And

Anatolia in the 11thcentury - the Seljuq Turkish. After being brought in in 1058 as mercenaries, they took control of Baghdad's Abassid dynasty and seized most of Anatolia, which was under the Byzantine Empire. In addition, they conquered the majority of the Levant. This was part the original purpose of their mission to defeat the Fatimid new dynasty Egypt.

Even at its height the Seljuq Empire was without a strong infrastructure, and it existed in a constant state of war. Syria, in Western Levant had squabbling leaders swearing allegiance only to Baghdad. This organization soon began to crumble, as was Palestine. Alexius Comnenus (1056-1118), Byzantine Emperor saw a way to regain some territory following the empire's decline. Frankish mercenaries had been employed by him in the past, so he wrote to Rome asking for more. The surprise was in the Pope's response. He called out for something new, a crusade.

It's also unclear how Pope Urban II came up with this idea of a Crusade for the Holy Land. Gregory had already called in 1074 for the "milites Christi," (soldiers Christi) but it had been ignored. Urban might have known about the Muslim concept or holy war of jihad. Also, the idea of aggressive expansion via holy war was not new to Christians during that period. Urban's idea was so original that he gave a speech to call his audience to go on crusade to Holy Land to win Jerusalem and wipe out the Muslim threat. Urban used a letter from the Byzantine Empire as an excuse.

He probably didn't know he would get the response he got. It was unprecedented. His goal was perhaps to at least gain some mercenaries, donations and even an armoured force to send to the Emperor. He did not just speak spontaneously, but he planned his speech carefully, maneuvering to bring leaders of the Crusade before announcing.

Urban spoke to Clermont, France's large population on November 27th 1095. This was known by the Council of Clermont. It was about Alexius's letter. Urban briefly warned against the violence of the knights. Urban himself was nobility. Urban also reported that the Seljuqs have conquered Romania and are attacking Europe as far west to Greece. He painted a picture illustrating Christianity under threat from this new Turkish threat.

Urban's actual speech has not been found, but several chroniclers described the structure and tenor of Urban's speech. Even those that were finished at the same time were written after Jerusalem was lost to the crusaders. Baldric, of Dol's, (c.1050-1130), Historiae Hierosolymitanae, libri IV Guibert, of Nogent,' Dei gesta for Francos

("God does deeds through Franks") Robert the Monk's (d.1122), Historia Hierosolymitana Fulcher, Chartres' chronicle and the anonymous Gesta Francorum, (Deeds from the Franks), comprise the crusade.

Figure of Pope Urban II presiding at the

Council of Clermont.

Fulcher de Chartres reports that the pope said that "I" or rather the Lord beseech you, as Christ's shepherds, to publish it everywhere and to persecute everyone of any rank and foot-soldier, knight, rich and poor, to immediately carry aid to Christians in need and to exterminate this vile race, from the lands and lands of our friends. I am not speaking only to those who can be present. It is also meant for all who cannot be present. Fulcher, Chartres and Urban II will continue:

"All who perish by the way of the pagans (either by land, sea or air) shall be forgiven their sins immediately. This I grant them with the power of God which I have been invested. What a shame that such a despised, demon- worshiping race should be allowed to rule over a people who believe in the omnipotent God and are made glorious with Christ's name! How will the Lord overpower us if you don't aid those who believe in the Christian religion? Let those who have been habituated to unjustly wage private warfare on the faithful now oppose the infidels. This war should have been won long ago. Let those who for a while were robbers now become knights. Let those who were fighting against their relatives or brothers fight now against the barbarians. All those who have been working as mercenaries to get a small amount of pay should now be rewarded. It is now up to those who have worn themselves out both in body as well as soul to earn a double omen. Behold! You will see! Don't delay your journey. Rent your lands to cover your expenses and when winter ends, get on with the journey.

Depiction Pope Urban II

The campaign attracted thousands with different agendas. The warrior classes were ready to fight. That was their bread and butter. The crusade offered them an unprecedented level of freedom and they didn't want to leave. Their violence was not restricted by their normal employers. Nor did they have the risk of losing any of these territories.

The Church, just like Urban's predecessors Gregory VII was ready to accept the challenge. European Christians were brainwashed to hate heathens with "irreligious" behavior.

Feudal Europe created the "primogeniture" program, which allowed the firstborn sons to inherit the patriarch's titles. This may have provided a solid foundation for the futures and health of the eldest males in European families. However, the second sons and others were left with no option but to look for other ways to survive, unless the firstborns were sickened by the plague or any other illness. Entrepreneurial people set up businesses and found ways to make a living. Many went on to become mercenaries, hired guns, and knights. These were the same men who made up the bulk crusaders.

Other reasons for enlistment included many and varied. Younger sons were eager to discover new lands, and get new properties that they could call theirs. Some saw this as an opportunity to expand their horizons. Though it might not be the best, the adventure of sailing across the open seas was enough to get many people excited. Kings arrested ungovernable and rogue knights looking to indulge their bloodlust. They rerouted their kleptomaniac urges towards enemy troops, villagers and soldiers.

Medieval folks used a figurative weight scale to measure their salvation. One side weighed in one's righteous deeds and the other one one's wicked ones. Whichever side weighed more indicated salvation or damnation. In this light, the Catholic mentality held that all it required to enter heaven was to make a score. This meant that "righteous works" such as pilgrimages and obedience to papal orders, could be enough weight to allow for entry to Heaven. Many of these sinners, especially knights/warriors who had suffered many losses, were the first to sign up for the enlistment. Urban had assured them that they would immediately be forgiven for their sins if they died on the battlefield against the Muslims, either by land or water.

These knights were from all walks. A cross was placed on each chest to prove their love for Christ.

Urban's famous speech had been a year in the making. In August 1096, four armies consisting of crusaders and each led by a different European leader, set sail to the Byzantine regions. To gain fame and glory, the more eager and less experienced army of Peter, the Hermit, left about a month earlier than the rest of the crusaders. Peter's troops arrived at their destination to be welcomed by more experienced Muslim forces and extinguished in Cibotus. Soon after arrived the crusaders and Count Emicho. They continued to wreck havoc on the Rhineland Jewish communities. Urban was surprised when Emicho's disobedience resulted in the killing of hundreds innocent Jews.

The terrible consequences of Peter & Emicho's insubordination were precisely the reason why each of 4 crusader armies pledged loyalty to the pope. None of them, except Bohemond of Taranto, did so. The delay proved worthwhile as the crusaders stormed into Nicea - the Seljuk capital of Anatolia - in May 1097 and had their flags erected by the end of June. Theirs was Antioch in Syria one year later.

Following their success, the crusaders decided that it was time to move on to the main event and set sail for Jerusalem. They confronted the Shi'ite Islamic callipte, better known by the "Egyptian Fatimids," and halfway through July 1099 the locals gave in. To the delight of the crusaders Jerusalem was now theirs once again, closing out the First Crusade. However, Tancred - Bohemond's nephew - had said to the Muslim leaders he would spare the people. Unfortunately, hundreds upon hundreds of innocent people, including children fell to the cross-crusaders' swords before the end, leaving a bitter taste in Muslim lips.

Medieval portrayal of the Siege of Jerusalem

The Crusader States

Contrary what Muslims think of the Crusades today, Islam in contemporary times was not affected or disturbed by them. The First Crusade was particularly unfavorable to Muslim chroniclers. They found the Muslim response scattered across various histories of greater concerns.

There were many reasons for this. First, Palestine existed between the Abbasid Seljuq Kingdom of Baghdad in Iraq and Egypt's Fatimid Empire. Many Muslim sources, including later ones, were unclear about the Crusaders' origins. The two empires were not one cohesive entity, but rather a series of squabbling city rulers that existed in an unstable and constantly shifting set alliances and rivalries. There was no consistent Muslim loyalty or alliance. And there was no Pan-Arab, let's not even Pan-Muslim, identity. Ibn Al-Athir for example believed that Franks were hired to be mercenaries by Fatimids against Abbasids, and not by Byzantines.

The religious motive behind crusade's execution was often ignored.

Another important reason that the First Crusade didn't get much attention from Muslim writers was that they were mostly Arabs. However most of those who wrote the chronicles were Arabs. The armies that Crusaders fought, however, were Turkish armies fighting in the interests of Turkey. The Seljuqs had displaced the Arab elites so there was a disconnect from the damage the Crusaders were causing to individual rulers as well as the concerns of those who recorded the events. Contrary the Frankish or Anna Comnena from the Byzantine, the Arab historians didn't feel any personal involvement and therefore did not give it much importance.

Perhaps most importantly, the Crusaders failed to pose a threat to the Muslim power centers by passing through the territory of Palestine or western Syria. The Crusaders didn't pose any threat to distant power centers such as Baghdad or Cairo. This attitude would not change for several decades.

Many crusaders travelled home, still on high from a victory that was much earlier than they expected. A small number of crusaders returned to their homeland to take over the management of newly conquered territories. Their rule lasted 45 years. In 1144, Zangi, the general from Mosul, and his soldiers broke through Edessa's border unannounced to seize the state.

The loss Edessa made it difficult for European Christian leaders to rebuild their egos. Three years later, Pope Eugene III urged for a Second Crusade. These campaigns were first to be managed by monarchs: Conrad III of Germany and Louis VII of France. Conrad, a crusader under Conrad, marched into Dorylaeum. This was where they had been victorious during the First Crusade. Conrad & Louis then consolidated at Jerusalem their forces and headed for Damascus (Syrian-owned Damascus) with an army of more than 50,000.

While the crusader armies might have been impressive, they could not match the Turkish forces. Zangi, Nur al-Din's successor, had asked for additional reinforcement. By 1149, all crusaders had been driven out of Damascus. Thus ended the Second Crusade. 5 years later was the transfer of authority over Damascus to Mosul.

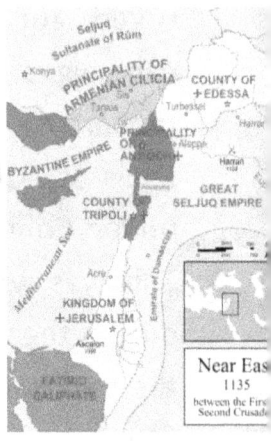

In 1187, the wounds suffered by the crusaders after their defeat were reopened. Saladin, the sultan from Egypt and the originator of the Ayyubiddynasty (also known as Saladin), and his troops crossed Jordan into the Kingdom. Saladin was commissioned to besiege Tiberias Fort. At the crusader base, leaders met to discuss tactics that would overcome the increasing threat from Saladin. The crusaders, despite their large army, fell into the Saladin trap due to their wrong calculations.

To stop Saladin and his men in Tiberias from being repelled, the crusaders had the to endure a 12 mile trek. This was made more difficult by the fact that they were dehydrated, had limited supplies, and the relentless heat. The crusaders stopped at Hattin to rest, but it was too late. The alarmed crusaders discovered Saladin's forces had already defeated them to victory and were standing guard above the Sea of Galilee. Saladin's men opened an ambush upon the frail crusaders. Guy of Lusignan - the king in the now collapsed crusader state Jerusalem - was among the ones captured.

Saladin went on his quest for more territories along the Levantine coastline. In the next 2 months, he added Acre (Nablus), Sidon, Jaffa Toron, Ascalon and Acre to his expanding empire. Saladin's

September 1187 goal was to capture Jerusalem. He led his troops toward the gates. The ensuing battle lasted for 10 days and was sparked by crusaders who made a desperate attempt to stop the invading forces. Bailan de Ibelin, who had been appointed in his absence as the king's command, raised the white flag. Jerusalem was under Muslim occupation as of October 4, 201187.

Tensions between Christian-Christian powers and Muslims were high. Therefore, it was critical to revamp the Outremer army. Many men from diverse backgrounds offered their help. The main class comprised the knights with their tenants, which included barons (bishops), bishops, and abbots. The knights referred to not just armored horsemen, but fighting units consisting of individual horse-mounted soldiers and their squires. This was a knight-in-training who served their superiors. Vassal warriors were those who received land as a reward for their military service. Retained or household knights, on the other hand, were men with no land and who were paid yearly salaries. These salaries could either be converted to food, clothing or other valuable resources.

Pilgrims also made up the core of Outremer armies. These pilgrims were either lured in by religious fast talkers, particularly during "Pilgrim Month" between April-October, or motivated by the cause. One of the most important pilgrim recruiters was Philip from Flanders, who arrived in Acre at 1177. His army featured several earls from Meath and Essex as well other high-ranking members in the English upperclass.

Mercenaries and other experts in the battlefield were hired in huge numbers to replace untrained farmers. These trained men were required to operate crossbows with other advanced weaponry and to lead what would otherwise had been a bandless farmers in armored suits. Many of these farmers were servitors, indentured laborers, and serfs. If they joined the crusade, they were promised their freedom. Turcopoles are a group of Christian converts with Arabic roots. Tucopoles could be freed from other crusader States who had grudges against Turks over heavy taxes and other injustices.

The last, but not the least, was the fighting monastery. These militant orders were started with the sole mission of defending Jerusalem and its Christian pilgrims.

Teutonic Beginnings

"Heal those in need, raise them up, cleanse leprosy-afflicted people, drive out the demons." Matthew 10;8

You can better understand the origins the Teutonic Knights by looking at its ancestor. Pope Gregory I, in 600 CE, appointed Abbot Probus as his architect to build a small Jerusalem hospital that could cater to the needs and pilgrimages of Christian Christians. The hospital survived for just four centuries. It was destroyed by fire during one of the sieges of the Holy City.

A medieval depiction shows Pope Gregory I dictating Gregorian chants.

Christian merchants from Amalfi in Italy built a Benedictine Benedictine Abbey in the holy city to pay tribute and honor St. John. The Caliph Ali az-Zahir, Egypt's Caliph, gave permission to resurrect it in that year. Gerard Thom was granted the blessings of Pope Paschal I in 1113. This was just 14 years following the First Crusade.

It took a tremendous effort to rebuild the infirmary. The vast interior was large enough for 2,000 patients to be accommodated, each with their own individual bed. There were 11 different wards. Some wards were intended to be used only by women and children. Each ward was manned daily by a brother and four physicians and 4 surgeons. Patients could enjoy clean and well-maintained facilities as well as freshly prepared meals and advanced medical treatment. They also had 24-hour access to care thanks to natural lighting and plenty of windows. The Hospitallers accepted patients from all walks of life, not just those who were pilgrims. Some of the staff may have even offered special meals to patients from "rivaling" faiths.

Raymond du Puy de Provence, the next in line to establish a new office near the Church of the Holy Sepulchre was the next. Under Provence's leadership, the Hospitallers were transferred from Benedictines over to Augustinians. He helped secure new lands for their hospitals

and strengthened the order's treasury.

Also, mercenaries could be hired to provide security at hospitals and to act as guards for non-packing monks as well as Christian pilgrims. The charity organization was now a military organisation, which led to the Knights of the Order of St. John the Hospitaller. Although they were armed but were monks by heart, the Hospitaller Knights were not able to leave their homes without taking vows of obedience, poverty, celibacy, and fidelity.

The distinctive black surcoats the knights of the order wore to distinguish them were made from loose-fitting robes with armor. A white Maltese cross was also splashed across each chest. The cross was distinguished by its distinctive inverted arrowheads that replaced its arms. It symbolized "our Savior's saving death, resurrection" and the 8 points the Hospitaller knights had to live by. They pledged to "live in truth", "have faith; repent their transgressions; show proof that they are humble; love justice; do good; be merciful; remain sincere and wholehearted;" and, finally, "endure persecution."

The Order of St. John was quite a different concept than the fledgling one it started from at the beginning of the 12th century. At this point, there was a clear boundary which defined the dominions among the Hospitaller orders' monks & knights. The structure was divided into priories. Next, a subdivision of bailiwicks was made, which was then further branched to become commanderies. They were exempted and taxed from civil duties and taxes. The Pope granted them special privileges, such as the right of building their own churches and other religious buildings. Frederick Barbarossa (the Holy Roman Emperor) protected them from any other authority than His Holy Holiness. Hospitallers and Knights Templar facilitated the constructions of numerous Christian fortifications in gratitude. The Order of St. John was permitted plenty of room to flourish, and it did so, planting seeds in many crusader nations. The Order of Saint John held 7 forts in their peak and over 140 other territories across the Outremer, including Antioch's Krak des Chevaliers and Margat.

Following Saladin's overthrow of the crusaders, which saw Jerusalem's Kingdom dwindle to only one base at Tyre (apparently incomprehensible but still a stronghold), Christian morale fell to its lowest point in a long period. Legend has that Pope UrbanIII died shortly after being informed that the Holy Land would no longer be held by the "barbarians". The Christian leaders were determined and determined to get over the stumbling block. Before long, Pope Clement III began a new war against "infidels," which triggered the Third Crusade.

France, England. Germany and the Low Countries offered their support immediately to the reawakened cause. Warrior spirits across the globe were called to "take" the cross, which was medieval slang and meant to refer to the oath that knights took to travel from Jerusalem, expel Saracens, restore the Holy Land under Christian authority. For even more rumors, some of which were fictitious and besmirching Islam's name and followers, it was a breeze to rally the troops.

Saladin, just a few month into the Third Crusade's third crusade, noticed that cracks were breaking the Christian resolve in 1189. The Christians, also known as the "Franks," were looking for a scapegoat for the Hattin disaster. Saladin cut his beard and ordered the confused subordinates of his former King of Jerusalem to release him. The sultan hoped Guy would return to Tyre, adding to the already chaotic atmosphere. Saladin predicted that Guy would return from Tyre to claim his crown, which he did. Conrad gave Guy a brand new crown, but he quickly booted Guy from the premises and bolted him out.

Guy was humiliated and sought revenge. Guy was able to find a small army with 400 horsemen as well as 7,000 foot soldiers. His wandering eyes landed on Acre. It was located at the tip of the Mediterranean Sea, and was famous for being the centre of maritime trade. Guy would find this the best place to restore his status. Guy and his pitiful forces were seduced by the potential wealth found there. They made their way towards Acre, marking their territory about a half-mile from Acre's gates. From there they built a small fort complete with a moat that was filled with water from nearby creeks.

Saladin at first was amused by Guy's gall and allowed his ex-king and soldiers to play house near Acre's gate. But, it was Guy's excessive confidence that caused his downfall. Saladin might've had a chance of survival if he had not taken the opportunity to gather troops from Egypt,

Dujar Bakr, and Sinjar upon learning about Guy's arrival. Saladin had finally gained control of his backup troops, from Egypt, Dujar Bakr, Sinjar, and Mosul. European reinforcements already began to occupy one beach in the south, along with the plains in northern and eastern parts of the city. Acre's docks were overflowing with what a witness called "tangled heaps" of Christian vessels. It was evident that Frank's threat wasn't a joke. Their troops now numbered 2,000 horsemen with 30,000 foot-trained soldiers.

Guy and his men held firm for 2 years as Saladin's soldiers tried to thwart them. Crusader armies, supported by Kings Philip II, Richard I and Austrian Duke Leopold V, docked ships in the already-crowded bay in July 1191. The cramped bay made it difficult for anyone to breathe, which only exacerbated the conflict. Instead of working together for a common goal

Christian leaders began to fight amongst each other, leading to a flood and eventual the assassination or retaliation of King Conrad.

King Richard stopped the madness in August 1192 when he defeated Saladin's forces in Jaffa. Richard and Saladin made a reluctant peace treaty one month later. They stipulated that Christian pilgrims should be permitted to return home from Jerusalem and that Richard would dismantle the fortifications at Ascalon. The Third Crusade was over once the ink was dried. Even though they could not recapture Jerusalem, Christians rejoiced because they had destroyed Saladin's empire. It was even better that they had laid the foundations for an Acre Christian kingdom.

The Teutonic tale would begin in September 1190 during the Acre chaos. Barbarossa sent 55 German vessels to assist Guy with Acre's capture. Some men from Lubeck-Bremen were among the passengers, while Master Sibrand was their commander. Master Sibrand's name may ring a few notes, as he's one of several assassination targets featured in one installment of the video game series Assassin's Creed. While Sibrand is described as a tall, broad-shouldered man with sandy hair and a slicked, sandy-blond complexion, the designers conjured up a different image. Sibrand, and many of the characters in early history of Teutonic Knights, remain shrouded in mystery. Guy or one among his aides only mentioned Sibrand in a 1190 document.

Sibrand was granted ownership of a plot next to St. Nicholas Cemetery. There he and his associates began to build a hospital. They were forced to invent as they didn't have any building supplies. Timber was taken from the frames of ships to make walls. The thickest sail that they could find was laid over the walls and used for a roof.

Sibrand's was not a German-built hospital in Middle East. The honor went to the one built by a wealthy German pilgrim crusader. It was constructed between 1120-1128. After welcoming ailing and injured pilgrims to his house at first, he began to accumulate a clientele and purchased a piece land in the Holy City. He then built his own hospital. The unnamed Good Samaritan originally paid for the hospital out of his own pocket. But when he couldn't pay the bills anymore, he started raising funds from local merchants and fishing for patrons back in the home. The 1187 fall of Jerusalem resulted in the destruction of his hospital. Unfortunately, these efforts by this Samaritan ran out of steam. Sibrand and his descendants would go above and beyond their expectations.

Sibrand's Hospital in Acre was built to honor the Blessed Virgin Mary. German soldiers who were wounded by the cross-cultural language barrier often had to manage their own affairs. Sibrand's staff soon expanded with more aid from those who had come from the motherland. They modeled their lives after the Order of the St. John Hospitallers of Jerusalem. Like the Hospitallers they had knights who looked after the hospital. But, they were still open to the idea of creating an identity for themselves.

From that day on, they called themselves the Hospitallers of the Blessed Virgin or the Order of the House of St. Mary of the Germans. Saint Elizabeth of Hungary would later become their second patron. She is best remembered for dedicating her life to the poor and dying to provide care for the neglected.

When former employees who had been ousted from Jerusalem following the destruction of their hospital joined the roster of Sibrand's new, but promising institution, the growing body of the soon-to-be-brotherhood took it a step further and renamed themselves the "Teutonic Knights of the Hospital of the Blessed Virgin Mary." The new order was inaugurated on November 19, 1190 by Barbarossa's son, Duke Frederick II of Swabia, and when the city fell into Christian hands, they were gifted with a permanent location in Acre. It would be another year until Pope Clement III recognized this order in Quotiens posteratur. This formal name is the Ordo Salutae Marie Teutonicorum. The Latin word Teutonic means "German origins".

A medieval painting of Duke Frederick II Swabia

The brotherhood had 40 knights when the order was officially recognized. The majority of them were noble-born and all pure German. Heinrich von Walpot was made the first Hochmeister (Highmaster), or Grand Masters of the Teutonic Order after the brotherhood received its credentials, certifying that it was a papal-backed religious/military order. Walpot, a Rhineland-born West German, was presented with a crude lump coal. However, he held it close and promised to do all that he could in order to make it the shining gem he hoped it would become. In 1199, he created the first batch of laws for his order. It received the papal seal of approval in Innocent III's Sacrosancta red romana bull in February the same year. The first structure of power was introduced by the statutes for the order. It contained only 2 classes of members - the priests, and the knights. Both were required to make the same vows of purity and to protect Christians from idolaters.

8 years after the start of the 13th centuries, Walpot died. Otto von Kerpen replaced him, who is believed to be another Rhineland citizen. The second Hochmeister's reign is unknown. However, it is believed to have been as rocky as it was short-lived, since the Teutonic and knights Templar started to tussle. In Acre, brawls became so regular that they were even visible in broad daylight.

Kerpen, who had just settled into his post, suddenly began to croak in the early 1209, and his reign was stopped in less then a year. Heinrich von Tugna, the third Hochmeister suffered a very similar fate and died shortly before 1209. His reign was shorter than that of Kerpen's. Even so, it didn't seem that the deceased was much missed. Tuna was criticised for his inexperience as a novitiate and for only three months. Some others blamed him for incompetence. Tuna, according one of his successors could not assemble 10 knights with complete armor on a good, sunny day. Not even if his own life was at stake.

Von Salza and the State of the Teutonic Order

"Kill the whole lot, and God will sort them out." - Pope InnocentIII

Hochmeister's title may have seemed cursed. It was apparently lifted by Hermann von Salza (the 4th grand master), who would singlehandedly open a new chapter to the Teutonic historical book. Von Salza had the ability to see clearly, was organized, and was very well-prepared for his job.

Jan Jerszynski's photo of Von Salza's monument at Marienburg Castle

Thomas Stegh shows the Marienburg Castle of Teutonic Order.

Salza was the child of ministeriales in Central Germany's Thuringia. His family were unfree knights, tied to the feudal and had an intense desire to find something more. He had always understood the importance of connections and spent his entire life nurturing and building relationships. He was never afraid to put in the hard work required and earned their trust through his diplomacy skills. He won more admiration than his superiors when, at age 19, he stood up for his countrymen, both at the Siege in Acre and the Crusade to 1197. Although the exact moment Salza entered that order has been lost in time, the 40 year-old Salza was awarded Grand Master status in 1210.

www.ingramcontent.com/pod-product-compliance
Lightning Source LLC
Chambersburg PA
CBHW050023130526
44590CB00042B/1787